RETIREMENT BY DESIGN

A Guided Workbook for Creating a Happy and Purposeful Future

Ida O. Abbott, JD

To Susan—
wishing you all the best—
Ida

Published in the United States by:
ULYSSES PRESS
P. O. Box 3440
Berkeley, CA 94703
www.ulyssespress.com

ISBN: 978-1-64604-021-6
Library of Congress Control Number: 2019951399

Printed in the United States by Kingery Printing Company
10 9 8 7 6 5 4 3 2 1

Acquisitions editor: Bridget Thoreson
Managing editor: Claire Chun
Editor: Renee Rutledge
Proofreader: Barbara Schultz
Cover design: Christopher Cote
Interior design: what!design @ whatweb.com
Interior art: page 40 © suesse/shutterstock.com; page 200 © Alexander Lysenko/shutterstock.com

CONTENTS

CHAPTER 5: **KNOWING WHO YOU ARE AND HOW YOU GOT HERE** **69**

CHAPTER 6: **THE IMPACT OF RETIREMENT ON YOUR RELATIONSHIPS** **106**

CHAPTER 7: **POTENTIAL FINANCIAL AND HEALTH CONSTRAINTS** **136**

CHAPTER 8: **GETTING YOUR LEGAL AND MEDICAL ARRANGEMENTS IN ORDER ... 156**

CHAPTER 9: **ENVISIONING YOUR FUTURE LIFE IN RETIREMENT ... 172**

CHAPTER 10: **ORGANIZING, PRIORITIZING, AND EXPLORING RETIREMENT POSSIBILITIES ... 215**

INTRODUCTION

> Above all, think of life as a prototype. We can conduct experiments, make discoveries, and change our perspectives...
>
> —TIM BROWN, CEO OF DESIGN FIRM IDEO

There is no one right time or right way to retire, but one thing is certain: Retirement is a major life change, and without preparation it can be highly unsettling. You know you should be planning for as much financial security as possible. But it is just as important to plan what you will do with your time for the rest of your life. You may have 20, 30, or more years ahead of you. You have spent decades building and enjoying your career. Leaving your job without something to look forward to can be jolting. But when you view the future as filled with promise and possibilities, and you have designed it on your own terms, the prospect of retirement can be exciting and revitalizing. The sooner you start preparing, the easier it will be to transition into an enjoyable and fulfilling retirement when the time is right for you.

Retirement is different from other career transitions. When you progress through a career, every new move builds on the last; changes keep you moving forward and upward, and you have some sense of what to expect in the next stage. Retirement represents the culmination of a career that has been at the center of your life and identity for decades. The future is entirely uncharted territory, full of unknowns and uncertainties, and without guideposts.

Planning for this next stage is a creative process that will continue and evolve over time. By starting right now to awaken your imagination and explore the many possibilities that will be open to you in retirement, you can lay the foundation to retire eagerly, happily, and with a clear vision in mind.

Most professionals do not plan for the life ahead; few even think about what they can do or want to do in retirement. They focus on the present, their work and their clients, and the routines of everyday life. Even in organizations with mandatory retirement, many fail to consider or plan for what's next. A survey conducted by Edward Jones found that more people plan for a two-week vacation than for retirement.

Consequently, many professionals who reach retirement age have not developed talents or cultivated interests outside of their work-related pursuits. They do not know where or how to begin planning for what they will do in retirement. Others have a multitude of interests and activities they can't wait to start. For them, the challenge is to set priorities, build a manageable schedule, and do what they want to do but at a comfortable pace. Still others find themselves retired due to external circumstances, not by choice. They may not have expected they would need to plan for retirement so soon. Whatever the situation that brings retirement planning to the forefront, people often don't know what questions to ask to get the process started, and they are unwilling to ask for help.

This workbook provides that help. It will show you how to design your life in retirement, what will fill the time, and what will bring you joy and fulfillment. It is intended to give you that guidance by asking questions that will help you start the transition process. This is what professional coaches do: they ask deep questions that help you discover your own answers. Paying close attention to your answers and reactions, and setting priorities and action items as you go, will point you toward options and possibilities that you didn't realize you had, or that you might never have thought about.

Some of the questions may make you uncomfortable. Thinking about the end of your career can be especially difficult when your personal and social identities are closely tied to your professional one. When who you are and what you do have jointly defined your identity for most of your life, that shift can be disruptive and emotional. When you retire, you may still think of yourself as an accountant, doctor, pilot, or executive, but others now see you as a "former" accountant, doctor, pilot, or executive, which carries a lower status. There is even a colloquial term for this shift: a "PIP" (or "FIP"), meaning a "previously (or formerly) important person."

In addition to losing professional identity and status, retirement can lead to the loss of vital facets of life: leadership positions, client relationships that have been nurtured for years, exciting and stimulating intellectual challenges, a place to go every day, and the community of people in your office and professional circles. It can signify the end of the professional road that you have spent a lifetime creating. Many professionals' lifelong interests and activities have revolved principally around their work; they have focused their careers on becoming experts who are indispensable to their organization. Retirement raises the prospect of becoming unimportant, obsolete, useless, bored, and financially insecure. Plus, it forces you to confront your own aging and mortality.

This bleak perspective explains why many professionals avoid talking, or *even thinking*, about retirement. Some older people love what they do, remain highly productive and energetic, and want to continue with their career indefinitely. But many people keep working because they do not know what else they could do. They define their value and skills narrowly, as a law firm partner, a nurse, or an engineer; they cannot envision other possibilities and the prospect of life in retirement is unknown and scary.

It doesn't have to be that way. Retirement is a natural career transition. It puts you on the threshold of a new stage where you might start a new career, a new business, or a new hobby. The person you are now will be the same when you retire, but what you do with your time will be different. You can be lazy or hyper-productive, you can travel or stay put, and you can decide and act according to your own schedule. So, where do you start? You've come to the right place to find out.

HOW TO USE THIS WORKBOOK

This workbook is intended to help you plan your transition from your current career into a retirement of your own design. Depending on your age and situation, you may work your way through it in different ways. If you are in your 50s, you might take a leisurely approach to build a thoughtful strategy that can be activated whenever you are ready to retire. If you are in your late 60s or older, and retirement is more imminent, you might develop your plans more quickly. The same is true if you have retired unexpectedly because the choice was not your own. And if you have been retired for a while but want to think more deliberately about what you want to do over the next few years, the workbook can help you design a "new" retirement.

This workbook asks you many questions without offering answers; those will come from you. It will help you understand yourself better and see your options more clearly. It offers exercises to help you make sense of your past and envision your future. It suggests that you list action items based on ideas your answers inspire, possibilities you want to look into, or people you want to call for information or help. And it encourages you to return to these action items and exercises to revisit your choices and priorities, and adjust your plans whenever necessary.

To keep your ideas about retiring in one convenient place, you can answer the questions, complete exercises, and make notes right on the pages of this workbook. If you want more space for any of the questions or exercises, it might be helpful to have large surfaces to draw on, such as a white board or butcher paper, Post-it notes in different colors and sizes, and colored markers or Sharpies.

Although this workbook is filled with questions for you to answer, it is not a test, there are no grades, you will not "turn in" your answers to anyone, and you are not required to answer all the questions or any particular questions. As a self-coaching tool, this workbook poses questions to make you think deeply, spot issues, envision possibilities, and inspire action. But for many people, choosing your answers may be better done with the help of others who can give you outside perspectives, encouragement, guidance, and reality checks.

I encourage you to use the workbook in discussions with your spouse, members of your Personal Advisory Team (defined in Chapter 2), a mentor or coach, and anyone else who can be helpful as you prepare for and transition into this next stage of your life. This can produce greater clarity and lead to ideas and solutions you might not have thought of alone.

If you know other people who are thinking about or transitioning into retirement, you might also form a peer group. Meeting together regularly in a small group to discuss issues you are all dealing with is a good way to process your own thoughts and help your companions sort out theirs. You can use this workbook as a guide, designating sections or topics to be discussed at each meeting.

Each chapter deals with a different aspect of preparing for retirement. The chapters are arranged in a sequence that will first clarify what retirement means today; help you understand yourself and your personal circumstances; help you envision, generate, and test possibilities for the future; and finally, set priorities and create a dynamic plan. It is generally advisable to follow the sections in order, but depending on where you are in the transition process, some sections, questions, and exercises may be more helpful and relevant than others. Take a quick overview of the workbook before you start to familiarize yourself with what it offers. Then decide what you want to focus on and how you want to proceed. You can return to any part of it whenever your needs shift. Pages for note-taking are available throughout the workbook so that you can jot down your thoughts, ideas, and action items as they come to you, then refer back to them later.

At the end of this workbook you will find a list of Resources, including books, websites, research reports, newsletters, tools, and organizations that relate to the questions and topics presented in the workbook. These resources will help you learn more about subjects that pique your interest or find more in-depth help or information.

I hope that using this workbook will generate many exciting ideas and make you eager to enter this new phase of your life. Be mindful, though, that having lots of good ideas can be a trap. You may find yourself thinking and planning without actually making anything happen. The purpose of this workbook is not to encourage wishful thinking; it is meant to spark action. Use the following pages to record thoughts and to-do lists, but then follow through. Learn more about yourself, identify your interests, make connections, pursue opportunities, and move forward to a happy and fulfilling future.

 Introductory Exercises

1. What are your objectives in using this workbook?

---

2. If you look back a year into your retirement, what will make you feel you are transitioning successfully into the next stage of your life?

---

3. When using this workbook, you will be more productive and honest with yourself if you are fully attentive and relaxed. This can be hard if you are busy, rushed, and under pressure. Try to unwind before you start answering the questions or doing the exercises. Try one or both of the following very brief techniques to help you become more relaxed and mindful.

For each technique, find a quiet place to sit comfortably, free from distractions. If you are in an office or other hectic environment, shut the door and turn off your devices.

Technique 1: Set a timer for one minute. During that minute, close your eyes and focus on your breathing. Pay close attention to your breath moving in and out of your body. When the timer rings, open your eyes slowly.

Technique 2: Close your eyes and put one hand on your belly. Take a deep breath. Hold it for a few seconds and feel it in your body. Then slowly, say "relax" to yourself and exhale, letting your whole body relax, starting with the top of your head and moving gently through your body from there: your face… neck… shoulders… arms… hands… back … stomach… hips… legs …feet... all the way down to your toes. Let your body go limp, heavy, and loose. Imagine the stress draining out of your body, through your feet into the ground. Hold this relaxed feeling for as long as you like. When you feel calm, gradually open your eyes.

• • •

For verbal guidance to help you through these techniques please visit https://ulyssespress.com/rbd. You will be able to listen to directions and prompts while you close your eyes and relax.

CHAPTER 1

WHAT DO WE MEAN BY RETIREMENT TODAY?

> The old retirement dream was freedom from work. Perhaps the new retirement dream is freedom to work in new ways, to new ends, in a manner that's personally meaningful.
>
> —MARC FREEDMAN

Forget the traditional notion of retirement. It's unfairly loaded with negative implications. It suggests withdrawal from work and meaningful activity and evokes images of doddering old people whose lives are marked by irrelevance, boredom, or senility. Yet paradoxically, contemporary advertising associates retirement with wealth, leisure, and fun. Ads feature retirees laughing on golf courses or cruise ships and enjoying busy social lives. But neither of these images describes most older people today.

The whole concept of "retirement age" is an artificial social construct based on myths about "old age" that have little meaning today. It comes from the passage of the Social Security Act in 1935, which set the retirement age at 65 (later reduced to 62). At that time, the average life expectancy in the US was 61. Today people are living much longer. The average life expectancy is now about 79 (81.1 years for women, 76.1 years for men), and life spans are even longer for those in the top income brackets. If you are 60 years old today, you have a 50% chance of living into your 90s.

People are not just living longer; they are also remaining healthier and staying active, fit, and productive well beyond their 60s. While some functions might slow for some people, no specific age can be viewed as a natural "end point" for a person's ability to work. According to a 2018 survey by Transamerica Center for Retirement Studies, the vast majority of adults in the US, including nearly two-thirds of baby boomers, plan to work past the age of 65 or not retire at all. And it has always been common for lawyers, doctors, business executives, academics, and other professionals to work well into their 70s and beyond.

Consequently, retirement today doesn't necessarily mean withdrawing from work. In fact, transitioning from full-time career employment into full-time retirement is now the exception, not the norm. You can be retired from a career and yet still be working, full-time or part-time, for others or for yourself, for money or for nothing but the satisfaction it brings you. Leaving your job does not necessarily mean stopping your professional pursuits; you can remain involved in many ways in the established career that will always be a core part of who you are. For example, it is common to see retired lawyers working in pro bono legal clinics or teaching law school classes; retired doctors working in free clinics in inner cities or abroad; and retired scientists founding or advising start-ups. Many retirees also become entrepreneurs. The Bureau of Labor Statistics reports that people over 50 will start more businesses in the years ahead than any other demographic group.

Yet the negativity surrounding the concept of retirement and the emotional distress of being old enough to reach "retirement age" make it hard for some professionals to leave their jobs. That's why we need to reframe the notion of retirement to emphasize the opportunities it presents after a long and successful career. Retirement offers the chance to spend time doing what we want and living in ways that will engage us, keep us stimulated, and give us purpose.

Think of retirement as a gift: a chance to shift gears, explore interests, and pursue adventures that have long been deferred. Retirement allows you to make choices about what you want to do in the future without regard to meeting corporate goals, suffering through endless paperwork, being tethered to others' demands, learning complex new technologies, or maneuvering through office politics.

Emphasizing the positive features of retirement requires some mind-shifting. Rather than the "end" of a career, see it as the beginning of a new phase of life. Retirement presents countless choices in almost everything you do. This can be overwhelming—or it can be fun. You can become an adventurer, exploring and experimenting, or use your time to start a business, learn to play the piano, or care for your grandchildren. With a positive mind-set, you can design your retirement to suit yourself. You can take charge of your life, prepare for both foreseeable and unexpected problems, and minimize or even prevent unwanted outcomes.

People move into retirement in myriad ways. Sometimes they start using one approach then shift to another. Here are some common patterns:

- **Ease in.** Some people just want to relax. For decades, they have had busy schedules and worked extremely hard. Now they have the time to take it easy and do just what they want without feeling guilty about it. They might play golf every day or watch hours of movies on Netflix. They take each day as it comes.

- **Stay involved.** Many professionals want to stay active in their field but on a modified basis or in a different way. They might do occasional work for their firm or a free clinic, consult for another organization in their industry, teach a class, or mentor students through a professional association.
- **Start an encore career.** Many people want to keep working but not in the same field. They might become entrepreneurs, go into public service, or take a job in a field that interests them.
- **Seek new adventures.** Adventurers view retirement as a chance to try something completely new. They might pursue an unrealized dream or a recently discovered passion. They might travel to new places, write a novel, or take up a challenging sport.
- **Study.** Professionals like to learn, and there are any number of programs and courses in most communities and online that feed that desire. Many people study for the sake of learning, while others hope to acquire new skills in order to pursue new types of paid or volunteer work.
- **Search.** For many people, the best way forward isn't at all clear. They spend time exploring and experimenting, trying out new ideas to see what sticks. They might or might not find something to settle on. It doesn't matter; for them, the journey itself can be fulfilling.

In planning your retirement, you might choose to use one or more of these approaches or invent your own. What you decide to do is entirely up to you. *But start soon.* Much of your success in retirement will depend on how well you have prepared. Giving yourself ample time to prepare means there's no rush and there doesn't have to be a specific goal; you can move at your own pace in any direction that appeals to you.

Keep in mind that it is most desirable to enter retirement when you are mentally, physically, and financially sound. Life is messy, though; unexpected things happen. People sometimes find themselves pushed into retirement earlier than expected or their plans are derailed by situations that cannot be predicted or controlled. While you can create a plan for retirement that is picture-perfect, life is constantly changing and there will always be surprises. This is another good reason to start thinking about your interests, priorities, and options for life in retirement sooner rather than later. Even if you have to change course at some point, careful planning will allow you to build resilience and adapt more easily.

RETIREMENT DESIGN PRINCIPLES

Planning for retirement is different from any action plans you may have created before. The plans you are probably most familiar with are focused on achieving specific and concrete goals within a designated time frame. If you are someone who needs clear, structured goals, you can apply this traditional approach in planning your retirement. Similarly, if you have a specific goal or project in mind—like joining a nonprofit board or taking four big trips a year—the traditional plan you are familiar with may work well.

In that approach, you apply your expertise to the problem at hand in a linear fashion. You define the problem, set a goal, gather and analyze data, decide on a solution, implement that solution, then measure results. You follow these steps using the principles, knowledge, and patterns of thinking you have learned in your particular discipline. This approach works well when solving familiar problems, but when planning for something as novel and open-ended as retirement, it is limiting. When you use your professional expertise, you utilize what you already know, which gives you a feeling of mastery and comfort. But if you want to explore a wider set of possibilities, you need more than your current knowledge, technical expertise, and established mind-sets. Planning for a major life transition like retirement requires facing up to uncertainties and risks. It is unfamiliar and highly personal, and it requires finding possibilities that you may not even know exist.

Retirement planning is also a dynamic, ongoing process, so you can be less goal-driven and more fluid. Unlike planning for a long vacation or a promotion, this stage of your life may last decades. Over the days and years ahead, things will change, in both yourself and the world around you. In planning for the future at this point in your life, you can devote yourself to experimenting, exploring, and trying out different opportunities until you establish a pattern and mix of activities that feels right for you. If your aim is to have a retirement that is active, stimulating, and meaningful, you don't need a deadline or timetable, and you can change what "active, stimulating, and meaningful" means as often as you develop new interests or get bored with old ones.

Accordingly, this workbook uses an innovative approach to retirement planning inspired by the principles of *design thinking*, which is a process for creative problem-solving. Design thinking arose as a method of product design in the late 1990s and has been adapted to life design at the Hasso Plattner Institute of Design (known as the "d.school") at Stanford University.

In contrast to goal-focused problem-solving, design thinking starts with what you are thinking and feeling and what you need and want. It inspires you to expand your thinking, explore new ideas, push past obvious solutions, and create an innovative and flexible roadmap to the future. It does this in five stages: Empathy, Definition, Ideation, Prototyping, and Testing. These stages are nonlinear in that they do not have to follow in any particular order and you can work in two or more stages concurrently. Design thinking is also iterative, in that stages can be repeated whenever and as often as necessary to arrive at the best solution, which in this case is the best future life for you.

As applied to retirement planning, this is what happens in each of the five stages of design thinking:

1. Empathy: Design thinking starts with empathy because it focuses on understanding the user's needs and experience, not just their goals and solutions. When designing your future life, the user is you, and empathy means understanding yourself, or "self-empathy." This requires reflecting deeply and honestly about yourself, including what you are feeling, what is important to you, and what you want. Knowing who you are now is critical in deciding where you're going next. If you have a family, it is also vital to understand the perspectives of your spouse or partner and family members who will be directly affected by your retirement.

2. Definition: As you examine the insights and patterns that are elicited in stage one, the next stage is to define the desired outcomes of your retirement planning. Possible paths forward begin to take shape and you start to decide what the components of a happy retirement might look like for you.

3. Ideation: This stage of design thinking is often the most stimulating part of the process. It involves generating lots of ideas about retirement, seeking alternative ways to view retirement, and thinking up innovative scenarios for what you might do. It is a time to challenge assumptions (your own and others') about what you should or shouldn't do, or what you can or can't do, and to decide what you want to do, what you want to avoid, what possibilities you want to look into, and what will make you happy.

4. Prototyping: This is an experimental phase in which you start to sample the possibilities you generated in stage three. The point of prototyping is to try things out in the real world rather than simply assess them as ideas on paper. You experience prototypes through interviews, conversations, volunteering, taking courses, interning, shadowing someone, and any other actions that will help you determine whether an option that sounds good will in fact be a good fit for you.

5. Testing: Testing is the fifth stage but not necessarily the final one. Once you have experienced a prototype firsthand, you can decide whether it is right for you as it is, whether to refine it and continue, or whether you want to drop it and start over again with something else. You can try out one prototype at a time or several at once, so deciding to start again with another prototype is not a setback. Indeed, this retirement design process is intended to keep you returning to earlier stages, reflecting on your experiences, redefining desired outcomes, creating new ideas, and testing and refining prototypes until you achieve the best retirement possible. In a transition as open-ended and subject to change as retirement, this can be a lifelong process.

To give you an example, let's say you think it would be fun to travel when you retire but you are not sure where or how you'd like to go. You would start by first examining what you know about yourself as a traveler (*empathy*). What kind of trips have you taken before, what were your favorites, and why? Where have you always wanted to go, and what would you do if you went there? How much comfort do you prefer, and what can you afford?

Once you have that information, you can start to describe the places and kinds of trips that sound best to you (*definition*). You might infer that you prefer the idea of cruising to exotic destinations rather than flying to seven cities in 12 days, or you like backpacking in the wilderness more than visiting monuments and museums in big cities. Next, you can try to come up with lots of ideas for what a great trip might be (*ideation*). What appeals to you? Riding horses across Mongolia and living in yurts? Going on safari to luxury camps in Botswana? Buying an RV and driving to all the national parks?

The next step would be to try out some of these ideas, at least in a partial way, to see how you like them (*prototyping*). If you enjoy riding horses, you might arrange a pack trip at a dude ranch where you travel on horseback and camp in wide-open spaces. Before investing in an African safari, you could stay overnight at Safari West, a private wildlife preserve located near Santa Rosa, California, where you can sleep among the animals in tents imported from Botswana. Before you invest in an RV, you might take a bus tour to three or four of the national parks in Utah and see how you like the long drives between the parks.

When you take these "practice" excursions, you can check your hopes and expectations against a little bit of reality (*testing*). Depending on the outcomes, you can make better choices about your future travel plans. For instance, maybe you assumed you would prefer to do all the planning yourself, but after starting to research and organize a complicated trip, you might decide that an organized tour would be less stressful and more enjoyable.

If you are accustomed to the traditional step-by-step, goal-setting method for planning and problem-solving, this novel approach may seem vague or muddled. To fully benefit from it, you need to embrace certain essential mind-sets that will make it feel natural:

- *Curiosity*, which encourages you to be open to new ideas, invites you to explore and experiment, and makes things more interesting and fun.
- *Action orientation*, which commits you to doing something, not just thinking about it.
- *Reframing*, which expects you to examine your assumptions and biases, make sure you are working on the right problem, and keep moving forward.
- *Awareness* that you will sometimes experience setbacks, disappointments, and efforts that don't pan out, and that it is important to focus not on a particular goal or outcome but on the process of design and taking the next step forward.

- *Collaboration*, which emphasizes that you do not need to plan your retirement or go through your retirement transition by yourself, and encourages you to ask questions, seek input, and build a supportive team of advisors.

FINANCIAL PLANNING

One essential aspect of planning for the future involves finances. Most professionals appreciate the need for financial planning for retirement even if they don't do it. There are countless books, websites, articles, advisors, and other resources available to help you analyze your financial situation and plan for retirement, but this workbook is not one of them. You will find some basic questions about your retirement finances in the following pages, but they are not intended to serve as a substitute for careful financial planning.

To use this workbook most effectively, it is important for you to know what your retirement budget will accommodate, both short- and long-term. After all, unless you know what you will be able to afford today and in the future, your plans may not be realistic and your retirement may be disappointing or short-lived. If you have misjudged your finances, you may not be able to do many of the things you had planned to do; you might even need to return to work, which is harder to do the older you are. But if you have planned thoughtfully, you can build in alternative visions of retirement for different financial scenarios and more readily adapt your retirement plans if circumstances change. That's why it's best to take a close look at your entire financial picture as soon as you begin to contemplate retirement. If you have not yet done that, be sure to do it when (or even better, before) you start to use this workbook.

GIVE YOURSELF ENOUGH TIME

The act of leaving your job can be very quick—you just walk out of the building and close the door. But figuring out what to do in the months and years ahead doesn't happen that fast. And even if you have a plan of action, the psychological shift takes time. You will be entering a new stage and living a different life. If you are not emotionally ready for it, the change can be disconcerting and disorienting. In "8,000 Days of Retirement," its report about the four phases of retirement, Hartford Funds notes that two-thirds of new retirees struggle with the emotional adjustment to retirement. The good news, however, is that planning in advance for new routines, roles, and relationships can prevent these difficulties. The more time you give yourself to prepare, the easier it will be to adjust when you make the move, and the more excited you will be about forging ahead.

If you can start five years before your target retirement date, that is ideal. But the amount of time you will need to design and move into retirement depends on a host of factors, including your age, work situation, ideal (or known) retirement date, financial status, and personal circumstances, such as your family situation and health. Planning for retirement can begin at any age, and the younger you start the better. By using the design thinking approach presented in this workbook, you will be able to maximize your options and resources when you are ready to retire. And even then, it may take several months, a year, or more of transitioning before you hit your stride and settle into the roles, activities, and routines you feel satisfied with.

There is a popular movement among young people today called "FIRE," which stands for Financial Independence, Retire Early. These people are opting out of the workforce in their 30s and early 40s by radically reducing their expenses, saving as much as possible, and investing in income-generating assets. They leave their jobs at an early age but are only able to do it through careful and ongoing planning. Many people in their 50s are contemplating retirement from one career while planning an encore career, then expecting to retire again a few years after that. They might be planning two retirements at once. Some people in their 60s and 70s intend to retire at an age far in the future and can take several years to plan, while others find themselves out of a job unexpectedly and have only days or weeks. All of these people will have different timelines.

As a rule of thumb, give yourself more time than you think you will need. Even the best laid plans run into glitches that will delay or even derail your intentions. You might discover that you can't find a buyer for your business; the person you expect to take over your client relationships might leave the firm instead; or you might find it harder than you thought to hand over your job responsibilities to a younger, less experienced colleague.

Set aside some time dedicated to thinking, reflecting, and planning for your new beginning. Some people find it beneficial or necessary to get away and give it their full attention. They might take a mini-sabbatical or vacation for this purpose, or attend workshops and retreats that focus on making significant life transitions. Others set aside a little quiet time each week, maybe during morning walks or morning commutes.

The longer you give yourself, the more time you have to try out possibilities and come up with different scenarios. Let's say you plan to retire in two to three years. If you hope to enter a new line of work, you could lay the foundation for your move by doing a little work in that field while you continue your regular job. If you're thinking about moving to Belize and spending your days surfing and painting, you might spend a month living there and seeing how it works for you.

In addition to time for planning before you retire, allow yourself ample time to adjust once you have actually retired. You will be moving from a work environment that is structured, busy, and familiar to a life filled with new routines. You will need to find your footing, get comfortable with your new status, and face the many changes that retirement will bring. Even with advance planning and excitement about what's to come, it may take a while for you to adjust to this new reality. Most people take six months or more to become fully adjusted to retirement. So, go easy on yourself and stay focused on developing the plans and possibilities you have designed. The table below summarizes six factors to consider as you design your ideal retirement.

SIX KEY FACTORS FOR DESIGNING YOUR RETIREMENT

Retirement date	Set a retirement target date sooner rather than later. If your job has a mandatory retirement date, don't ignore it. Start planning for the transition at least a year ahead of your projected retirement date.
Age	The younger you are when you start planning your retirement, the more time you'll have to figure out what you want, try things out, and make wise decisions.
Finances	Your projected financial situation is critical to designing a successful retirement. The sooner you start financial planning for retirement, the more time you will have to maximize your retirement savings and assets.
Family situation	If you are married, your spouse's work and ideas about retirement must be part of your planning process. The ages and needs of dependent children, and your financial and support obligations to children and parents, are other factors that will impact the nature and timing of your retirement.
Current work situation	Your work situation is a determining factor in how much time you will need to develop and execute an exit strategy in order to retire and move on. For example, if you own your own business, how long will it take to sell it?
Health	You want to enjoy retirement in good health. If you know that your or your spouse's health condition will limit your retirement options, you might want to speed up your target date. In any case, take care of yourself. Exercise, eat healthy foods, manage your stress, develop other healthy habits, and have regular medical checkups.

Chapter Review

1. *Do you have a target date for retirement? How much time will this give you to design your retirement?*

2. *How will you set aside time to concentrate on planning your retirement?*

3. *What have you learned about yourself in this chapter? List your five most important insights.*

1. ______
2. ______
3. ______
4. ______
5. ______

4. *What do your insights suggest about your choices for your future retirement?*

5. *List three to five decisions you have made or are considering about your retirement, or about retirement planning, after completing this chapter.*

1. __________
2. __________
3. __________
4. __________
5. __________

Additional Notes and Action Items

Use this space to record additional notes or observations, as well as any action items they inspire.

CHAPTER 2

CHOOSING A PERSONAL ADVISORY TEAM

> If you want to go fast, go alone; if you want to go far, go together.
>
> —AFRICAN PROVERB

You may choose to use this workbook by yourself, but it is usually helpful—and sometimes necessary—to discuss your thoughts, needs, and concerns with one or more people. As you plan and go through your retirement transition, it will be important to have a Personal Advisory Team to inform, support, and encourage you. The team will likely take shape as you go along, but start now to think about who you might want to have on it.

WHO SHOULD BE ON YOUR PERSONAL ADVISORY TEAM?

Your team should include family members and friends who know you well and care about you, as well as others who know you in different ways and may have something of value to offer you, such as their own experience with retirement or ideas that may inspire you. They do not all have to be close friends, but they do need to be willing to be supportive and helpful.

If you are married or have a life partner, you have one team member already. After all, the changes that occur with retirement will affect both of you, and depending on your ages, you may be looking at 20, 30, or even more years together. Developing a common vision for the future requires early and ongoing communication. It also requires a willingness to be flexible, make compromises, and respect the concerns, interests, desires, and expectations of your partner.

Friends and colleagues who have retired successfully can be especially valuable team members. They can serve as your "retirement mentors," sharing valuable insights about what has worked for them, what has been difficult, and what they have learned. Talking with someone who brings a broader perspective and an understanding of what you are feeling and dealing with can reveal long-forgotten abilities and passions, lead to the discovery of unimagined possibilities, and reignite a sense of purpose and adventure.

The members of your Personal Advisory Team can be as varied as you want or need. You might consult some team members on a regular basis about many different issues, and contact others only occasionally for more circumscribed purposes. Possible team members could include:

- A professional retirement coach to guide and support you through the process.
- A financial advisor who can help you understand your finances, your future income and expenses, and how to budget for the plan you are creating.
- A close friend, therapist, or spiritual leader who can comfort you during times of anxiety.
- A physician who can give you guidance and advice about health management or a personal trainer who can provide discipline and support.
- Mentors you admire who know you well, who can offer you insights and advice in an honest and supportive way.

Identify Possible Personal Advisory Team Members

The process of building your Personal Advisory Team may take a long time. You can always add to your team as new needs or interests arise.

To help you identify possible members of your team, consider how each one can contribute to your exploration of possibilities and/or development of your plans for the future.

Who are the people most important to you?

____

____

____

____

____

Who are the people you are closest to?

On whom can you rely for support and encouragement?

Whom can you trust to be honest with you?

Who will be most affected by your retirement decisions and activities?

Whose expertise, experience, and advice would be especially valuable?

Who can offer assistance in specific areas you are concerned about, such as finances, health, or job possibilities?

Who can think creatively to help you generate new ideas?

____

____

____

Would it be useful to engage a professional retirement coach?

____

____

____

• • •

If you know your potential advisors well, it will likely be sufficient to ask them when you see or call them. If you want to invite someone you do not know well, you should first determine whether they can help you in the way you hope they will. You might schedule a lunch to get to know them better and ascertain their suitability and willingness to help you. If they do not live nearby, schedule a phone or video call. Be prepared with specific questions that will elicit information you need to decide whether to invite them to be part of your ongoing team. Be sure to explain (and limit) what you want from them and how much time you will need from them.

 Build Your Personal Advisory Team

1. *List your prospective Personal Advisory Team members on the table on page 28.*

Think carefully about why you have included each person on your list and indicate the kind of help they can best provide to you. Include people who have experience, expertise, and connections in areas where you don't. Be sure you have a diverse team in terms of the assistance, insights, and advice they can offer, the kinds of experiences they have had with retirement, and the type of relationship you have with them. When you reach out to them, explain what you are doing, why you selected them, and the kind of help you would like from them.

YOUR POTENTIAL PERSONAL ADVISORY TEAM

Name	Type of help desired	Date contacted	What did they say?

2. *Once you have contacted your potential advisors, jot down the individuals who will be members of your Personal Advisory Team.*

Remember that this team is not finite or complete. As your needs change or you get to know people who would be helpful or supportive, add new advisors to your team.

Members of Your Personal Advisory Team

1. ____________	7. ____________
2. ____________	8. ____________
3. ____________	9. ____________
4. ____________	10. ____________
5. ____________	11. ____________
6. ____________	12. ____________

Expressing Gratitude toward Your Personal Advisory Team

Unless they are professionals who are being compensated for their services (e.g., an estate planner), the people who agree to support you during your retirement transition will probably not expect anything in return. Nonetheless, if there is something you can do for them, they will be appreciative. At the very least, remind them of your gratitude. If you think some of your advisors would enjoy meeting each other, bring them together for breakfast or lunch and make introductions.

3. *Keep notes of what you learn from each member of your Personal Advisory Team. Copy the following template to record notes of your conversations with each team member and any ideas or action items they inspire.*

Team member name ____________

Date of conversation: ____________

Topics discussed: ____________

____

____

Conversation notes: ____________________

____

____

____

____

____

____

____

____

Ideas: ____________________

____

Action items: ____________________

____

____

____

____

Chapter Review

1. *What have you learned about yourself in this chapter? List your five most important insights.*

1. ____________________

2. ____________________

3. ____________________

4. ____________________

5. ____________________

2. *What do your insights suggest about your choices for your future retirement?*

____

____

____

____

____

3. *List three to five decisions you have made or are considering about your retirement after completing this chapter.*

1. ____________________

2. ____________________

3. ____________________

4. ____________________

5. ____________________

Additional Notes and Action Items

Use this space to record additional notes or observations, as well as any action items they inspire.

CHAPTER 3

EXPLORING YOUR ATTITUDES AND FEELINGS ABOUT RETIREMENT

> We must be willing to let go of the life we have planned, so as to have the life that is waiting for us.
>
> —E. M. FORSTER

Transitioning into retirement requires you to leave your career behind and move on. Some people have no trouble with this; they can't wait to retire! But many people, especially professionals, find it hard to leave what has been their life's work. Relinquishing that work, plus the prestige and compensation associated with it, may arouse strong emotions that make it hard to let go and move forward. However you feel about leaving your job, by taking the initiative to envision your future and create a plan for achieving it, you shift your attention and energy in a more positive direction.

This chapter helps you examine your attitudes and feelings about retirement. Understanding your emotions will make it easier to manage them and to deal with both the idea and process of retirement. The chapter also includes a mind mapping exercise to help you organize your thoughts about what you want to address as you design the various facets of your future.

YOUR ATTITUDES ABOUT RETIREMENT

It is important for you to express your feelings and attitudes about retirement. Those feelings and attitudes will directly affect how quickly, smoothly, and successfully you will be able to make your transition. Be honest with yourself. No one but you needs to see your answers, but it might be helpful to discuss your thoughts with a person you trust who can help you process some of the emotions that you uncover.

Reasons for Retiring

Why are you retiring?

Did any particular occurrence trigger your decision to retire? If so, what was it?

If there was a triggering event, how did it make you feel at the time? Have your feelings changed since then? If so, how do you feel now?

If there was a triggering event, are your feelings about the incident affecting your ability to move forward?

 Feelings about Retirement

What does retirement mean to you?

____

____

____

____

How do you feel about retiring?

Circle where you fall on the scale below (1 = excited, can't wait; 3 = ambivalent; and 5 = I dread it).

1 2 3 4 5

Explain your answer: ____

____

What emotions does the idea of retirement arouse in you? Circle all that apply.

Ambivalence	Envy	Resentment
Anger	Excitement	Sadness
Anticipation	Fear	Shame
Anxiety	Guilt	Shock
Calmness	Happiness	Sorrow
Confidence	Indignation	Surprise
Dejection	Joy	Worry
Dread	Pride	Other: ________
Eagerness	Rejection	Other: ________
Embarrassment	Relief	Other: ________

What excites you about retiring?

What are you afraid of?

What are you looking forward to when you leave your job?

What will you miss?

Do you feel ready to face the changes that retirement may bring? If not, what would it take to make you feel ready?

At work, your success could be measured by your title, compensation, and status in your field. When you are retired, how will you measure personal success?

____

____

____

____

ELIMINATING NEGATIVE MENTAL IMAGES AND DYSFUNCTIONAL BELIEFS

Many individuals find retirement planning difficult because their mental images and beliefs about retirement are negative. The following exercises will help you examine any pessimistic thoughts and reframe them to make them positive.

 Rebut Negative Mental Images

The mental images you hold about retirement can have considerable effect on your ability to embrace retirement. If you are bothered by negative images of retirement, list them and then disprove and rebut them by referring to your own life or to friends who are retired. A couple of examples are provided to help get you started.

Negative Mental Image	Rebuttal
Retired people are ...inactive	Retired people have time to do many interesting things. My retired friends John and Mary are good examples.
Retired people don't...have much to offer	I have a lifetime of valuable experience, know-how, and accumulated wisdom, and that won't change when I retire.

Negative Mental Image	Rebuttal

Reframe Dysfunctional Beliefs

Sometimes what holds people back from retiring are beliefs they hold about themselves, their options, or what will happen to them. One way to deal with dysfunctional beliefs is to acknowledge them, recognize that they are untrue and harmful, and reframe them into positive assertions.

Two common dysfunctional beliefs appear below along with examples of how they might be reframed. List and reframe some dysfunctional beliefs you hold that are impeding your movement forward.

Dysfunctional Belief	Reframe
I cannot retire because there's nothing else I know how to do besides my work.	I have many skills that can be applied in new contexts.
I can't afford to retire.	I will work with a financial advisor to come up with a retirement plan I can afford.

Dysfunctional Belief	Reframe

Your New Elevator Speech

During your career, you might have had to create an elevator speech, or a succinct reply to the question, "What do you do?" After you retire, how will you respond when someone asks you that question? Write your new elevator speech below. Frame it in a way that is positive and focuses on the present rather than the past in order to spark interest in the listener. Try starting with an introduction like, "I am embarking on an exciting new adventure," "I am completely changing my life," or "I am exploring the possibility of . . . ," and *not* "I am a retired X. . . ," "I was. . . ," or "I used to . . .".

____

____

____

____

____

 What Are Your Anchors?

Below is a picture of a boat with anchors tying it down. In each anchor, write something that is making it hard for you to move ahead with retirement. For instance, what is preventing you from:

- Leaving your job?
- Telling colleagues about your plan?
- Talking with your spouse about retiring?

Add more anchors if needed. Draw a line between each new anchor and the boat.

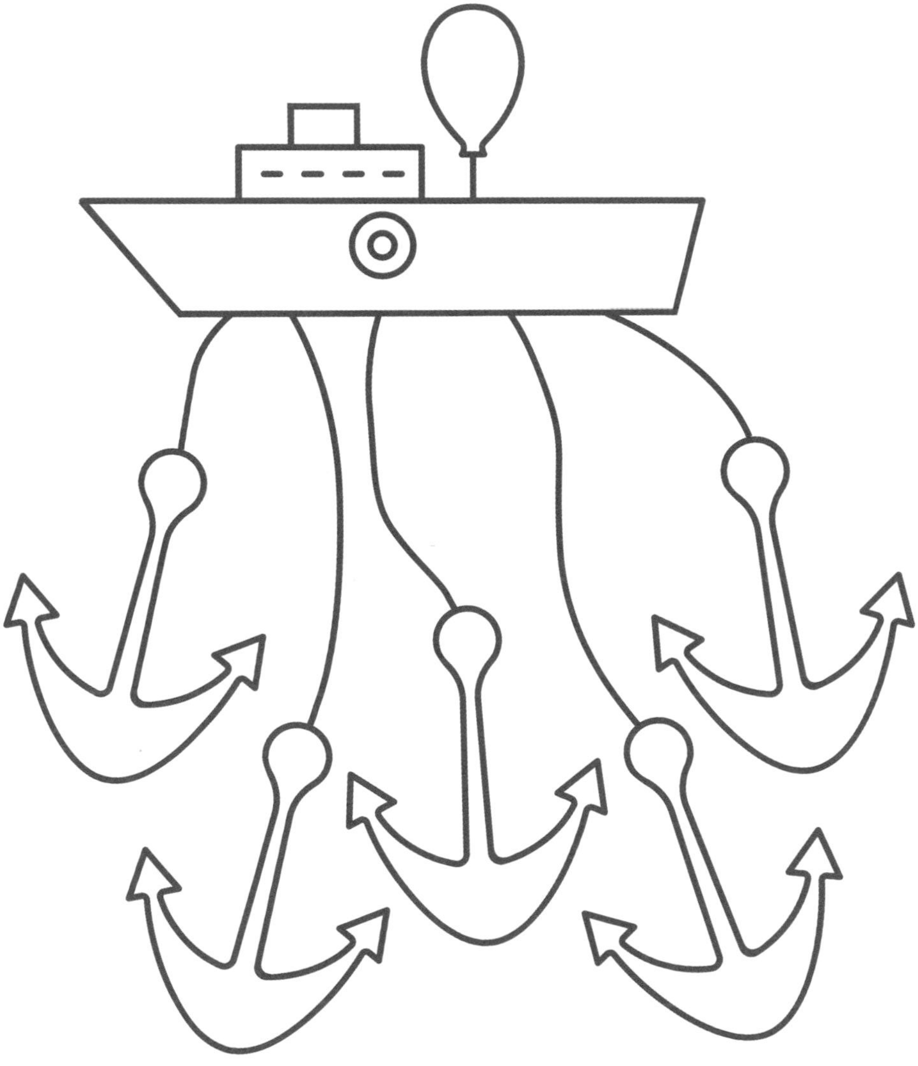

Now, imagine how much faster you could proceed if you cut yourself free from the anchors! To do so, think about the following:

- How can you detach your anchors? When you know how you'll do it, cross out each eliminated anchor.
- If you can't eliminate an anchor altogether, can you add a "buoy" or balloon above the boat to relieve the anchor's pressure and provide some lift to ease your movement? For example, if one of your anchors is not having enough money, maybe you can lift that anchor by reducing your expenses and living on a smaller budget. Write your ideas or action plans in balloons above the boat. One sample balloon appears in the picture. Draw and write in additional balloons and draw a line between each and the boat.

 Mind Mapping  

One way to start thinking in a positive way about what your retirement might look like is through mind mapping. A mind map is a tool that captures your thinking and presents your ideas in visual form. It is similar to taking and organizing notes, but because it is also visual and spontaneous, it encourages creativity and a freer flow of thoughts.

You can start mind mapping with a fairly specific problem, such as "when to retire," "encore career," or "where to live." Alternatively, you can start with a big concept like "retirement." If you start with a big concept, you might turn some of the subthemes you generate into separate mind maps.

Mind mapping literally allows you to map out your ideas. You will find space on the next few pages to map out some of your retirement ideas. If you need a bigger work space, you might want to use a large piece of paper, which will give you ample space to spread out in all directions and express yourself freely. You can find and use mind-mapping software online, but the tactile nature of drawing on paper can enhance the creative process. Using images and different colors can also enhance the experience. And remember, the point is to generate and connect ideas, not to create a work of art, so do not censor or hold yourself back by worrying about how it will look to others.

To show you what a mind map looks like, here is an example of a mind map for planning a party:

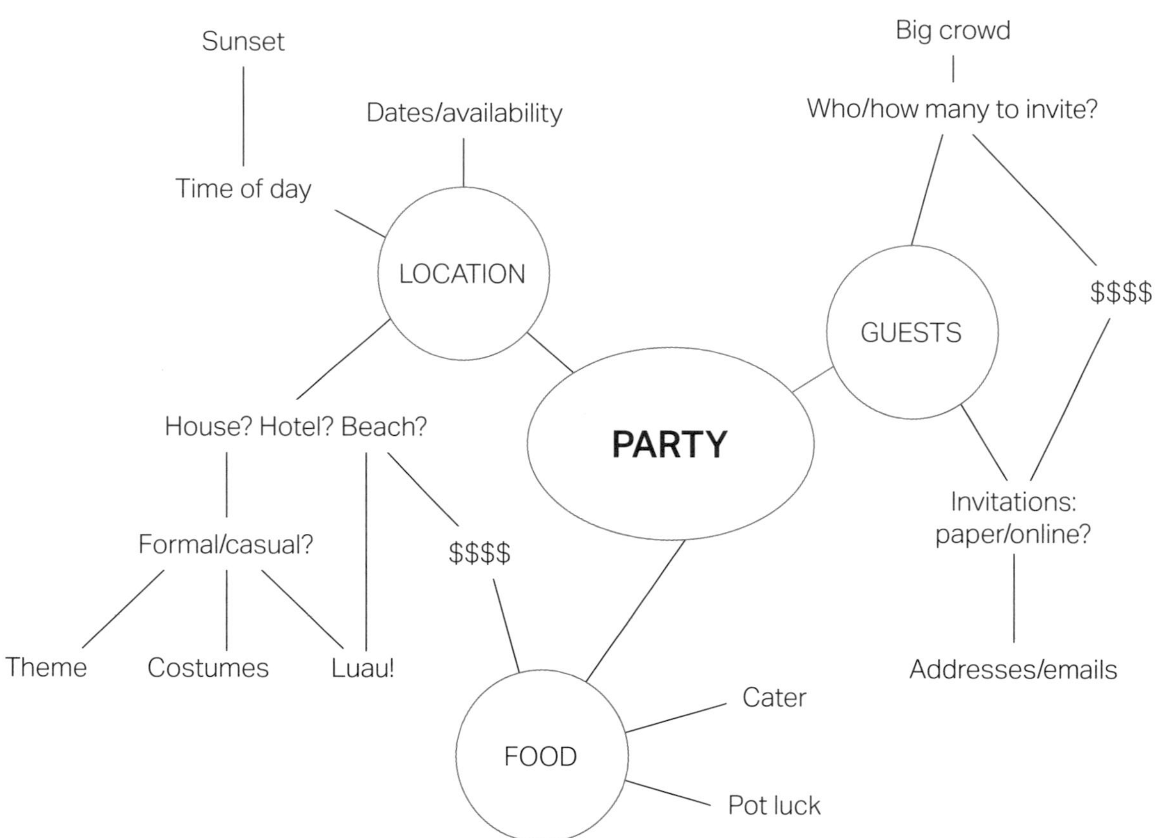

You can use the space provided on page 44 to draw your own mind map about retirement, or use a separate page of paper. To create your mind map:

- **Place a central theme in the center of the diagram and circle it.** Use a word and/or image such as "when to retire" or "where to live." This is the subject you will address. Other thoughts will radiate from this central theme.
- **What thoughts, words, or images automatically come into your mind that you associate with that central theme? Write down a key word for each of those subthemes around the central theme.** Connect them with lines to the central theme.
- **For each of these first-level associations, repeat the process.** Around or next to each subtheme, write down the key words you associate with it. You can repeat the process to third, fourth, or even fifth degrees. This should produce several subsidiary branches that radiate from your central theme and become more specific and detailed with each level.
- **Use only key words, images, and symbols, not sentences.** Use different colors. The map should reflect, visually and through words, many simple concepts that are connected with the central theme and with each other in various ways.
- **Work quickly.** Don't limit or judge your ideas before you write them down. You can analyze and refine them later.
- **Write down your ideas just as they come to you and in any order.** Don't worry about neatness or organizing them until after you have created the map.
- **Study the words and images on your map.** Highlight a few things that look most interesting or that seem related. See where you can find connections, patterns, and inspiration all over the map. Can you combine some of them into two or three ideas? Which ideas will you convert into action items?

SKETCH OUT A RETIREMENT MIND MAP

 Chapter Review

1. What have you learned about yourself in this chapter? List your five most important insights.

1. ______________________________

2. ______________________________

3. ______________________________

4. ______________________________

5. ______________________________

2. What do your insights suggest about your choices for your future retirement?

____

____

____

____

____

3. List three to five decisions you have made or are considering about your retirement after completing this chapter.

1. ______________________________

2. ______________________________

3. ______________________________

4. ______________________________

5. ______________________________

Additional Notes and Action Items

Use this space to record additional notes or observations, as well any action items they inspire.

CHAPTER 4

STARTING YOUR TRANSITION INTO RETIREMENT

We cannot become what we need to be by remaining what we are.

—MAX DE PREE

This chapter will help you think about the steps you will have to take to leave your current job and begin the transition into retirement. It will help you understand what that transition process might look like for you and issues that you should prepare for. The initial questions below apply wherever you work, while subsequent questions raise particular points to consider if you work as an employee, a partner, an individual practitioner, or a business owner. After you address the general questions that apply to everyone, you can answer only the questions that pertain to your specific work situation.

Your retirement process should also include identifying and grooming your successors so that your responsibilities and client relationships will continue to be handled seamlessly when you leave. Later parts of this chapter will help you organize and begin or complete efforts to prepare your successors and clients for your retirement.

Transitioning into Retirement from Any Workplace

Have you started to prepare for your retirement transition?

❑ Yes ❑ No *If yes, what have you done?* ______________________________

____

____

____

If you have not started to prepare for your retirement transition, what is preventing you from getting started?

____

____

____

How soon would you like to start transitioning into your retired life? Do you have a timeline or target date?

____

____

____

How quickly do you want to transition to a new lifestyle and schedule? Do you want to have a plan ready immediately, take some time off first to relax, continue working part-time for a set time period, phase out gradually without any timeline, or take a different approach?

____

____

____

Golden Gap Year

Some people who start to think about retirement take a "Golden Gap Year" to consider their next steps. Like the gap year that many young people take before starting college, this is a stretch of time to think about and explore what you want to do in the future. It is typically a journey that is beyond the usual vacation and involves new and different experiences like extended travel, a new line of work, or meditation and introspection. The gap experience provides an opportunity to try out various interests and ideas you are considering before you make any decisions. For example, you might find that after several months of traveling, you want to do even more, or alternatively, that you prefer to stay closer to home. Many people also find that their adventures spark entirely new ideas and take them in unexpected directions.

Would you like to take a break—perhaps a sabbatical or "gap year"—while you consider a possible future?

❏ Yes ❏ No *If yes, How can you make it happen?* ____________________

____

____

If you are subject to licensing and continuing education requirements, wlll you continue to maintain your active status as a licensed professional after you retire?

❏ Yes ❏ No

If you maintain your active status, what will that require you to do? Is there an option for you to stay licensed but become "inactive"? What would that mean for you in retirement?

____

____

____

Questions to Consider If You Are Employed by an Organization

If you work as an employee, consider the following questions to better prepare you for announcing your retirement. If you do not fall into this category, skip ahead to the appropriate section below.

Are you subject to an employment contract or retirement policy and, if so, how does it affect your retirement decision (this may be outlined in your employee handbook)?

____

____

____

____

How much advance notice must you give your employer before you leave?

____

Are there any provisions that worry you or create any difficulties for you?

____

____

____

Which clients or fellow employees will be most affected by your departure? Do you need to consider them in making your plans?

____

____

____

How will your retirement affect your 401(k), retirement plan, or pension benefits?

____

____

____

How will your retirement affect the life, health, disability, long-term care, or other insurance you receive through the company?

____

____

____

Are you entitled to be paid for any accrued vacation or bonuses?

❑ Yes ❑ No

Are you entitled to any career coaching to help you transition out of the company?

❑ Yes ❑ No

What terms regarding your retirement will you need to negotiate and what do you need to do to prepare for that negotiation?

____

____

____

____

Should you seek legal advice and/or representation regarding the negotiation?

❑ Yes ❑ No

According to your employee handbook, to whom must (or should) you give notice about your plan to retire?

Person to give notice to: ______________________________

If your employee handbook does not explain clearly whom you should notify about your plan to retire, or there is no handbook, have you told the people to whom you report?

❑ Yes ❑ No *If no, why haven't you?* ______________________________

____

____

____

How do you expect them to react?

____

____

____

____

Have you informed others in the company (e.g., colleagues, team members) about your plan to retire?

❑ Yes ❑ No *If no, when do you plan to talk with them? What will you tell them?*

____

____

____

Questions about Retirement for Members of Partnerships

If you are a partner in a partnership, these are questions to consider in advance of retirement.

Does your firm have a retirement policy? If so, how does it affect your decisions about your future?

If you are subject to a partnership agreement, does the agreement address retirement? For example, how much advance notice must you give the firm before you depart?

If you are subject to a partnership agreement or retirement policy, what does it say about future compensation, return of capital, pensions, 401(k) and retirement plans, and other financial provisions?

Does the partnership agreement or retirement policy address the effect of retirement on your life, health, disability, malpractice, long-term care, or other insurance?

How do the terms of the partnership agreement or retirement policy affect your decisions and plans for the future?

Are there any provisions that worry you?

In light of the firm's retirement policy and/or the partnership agreement, what terms will you need to negotiate?

What do you need to do to prepare for that negotiation?

Should you seek legal advice and/or representation regarding the negotiation?

Have you informed your partners about your plan to retire and, if so, how did they react? How did the discussion make you feel? Did it give you any reason for concern about your plans?

If you have not informed your partners about your plan to retire, why haven't you told them?

When do you plan to talk with them about your retirement and what will you tell them? How do you expect them to react?

Questions about Retirement for Sole Practitioners and Business Owners

The following questions shed light on the unique issues you need to consider as a sole practitioner or business owner prior to retiring.

Does your practice/company have a retirement policy? If so, how does it affect your decisions about your future?

Do you have an exit strategy for leaving? If so, describe it. Include how long you think the process will take and when you will begin the process.

____

____

____

What do you want to do with your practice or business? Wind it down? Sell it? Transfer clients to another person or firm?

____

____

____

What have you done to explore whether the option you desire is feasible?

____

____

____

If you have not looked into it yet, what steps must you take?

____

____

____

Have you informed your employees about your plans to retire?

❑ Yes ❑ No *If no, when will you do that?* ______________________

____

____

____

If you plan to sell your practice/business, have you had its value appraised by an expert?

❑ Yes ❑ No

If you plan to sell your practice/business, have you looked for a potential buyer or contacted a broker about finding a buyer?

❑ Yes ❑ No

Do you work in a field where there is high demand for your products or services but a shortage of providers with the ability and desire to take over your practice/business? If so, what can you do to find providers who have the necessary ability and desire? For example, have you investigated schools, professional associations, job fairs, colleagues in similar fields, media outlets, job search websites, or other sources of potential leads?

____

____

____

____

____

If you sell or transfer the practice/business to another person or firm, are you willing to remain as a consultant? If so, for what period of time? What financial arrangements will you want?

____

____

____

Do you want to transition out of the practice/business gradually? If so, over what period of time? What financial arrangements will you want? What other terms are important to you?

____

____

____

SUCCESSION PLANNING

When you retire, you want to be sure that the people, teams, and organization you leave behind continue to function well and give your clients the quality of service you have established. Identifying your successors is important so that you, your clients, and the organization can rest assured that the people who take over from you are competent and capable. Preparing your successors is essential so that the transition to new managers and leaders goes smoothly and without disrupting operations. Grooming your successors means that your institutional knowledge and professional wisdom will be passed along to those who assume your responsibilities. Readying your clients for your retirement makes it more likely that they will stay connected to the firm through the people who will take over when you leave.

Effective succession planning cannot be done at the last minute. Identifying and developing the right successors, providing them sufficient experience, transmitting knowledge, and transferring responsibilities can take many months or even years.

 Transfer of Leadership Roles

Does your firm/organization have a leadership succession process and, if so, have you reviewed the process and taken the steps it requires?

If you have started the succession process, list the positions of leadership or management responsibility you hold that need to be transferred to someone else. For each leadership or management position, name the successor you have started to prepare and describe what you are doing to groom that person.

Leadership Role	Successor	Actions Being Taken

If you are not yet preparing your successors, what must you do to identify and groom those people, and when will you start?

____

____

____

For each leadership role where your successor has not yet been selected, fill in the chart below. Indicate the possible successors for each leadership role, and the pros and cons for each candidate, including the factors that will help you decide their suitability and readiness for the role. In the last column, indicate any other individuals who should be involved in the selection process.

Leadership Role	Possible Successors	Pros/Cons	Others to Involve

Leadership Role	Possible Successors	Pros/Cons	Others to Involve

Once you select the successor for a leadership role, complete the chart below. List the role and successor, indicate what needs to be done by you and others to prepare the successor for that role, and state when you will begin the leadership transition process.

Role and Successor	What Needs to Be Done to Prepare Successor	Start Date

Transitioning Clients

Does your firm/organization have a client transition policy or process? If so, have you reviewed it and taken the steps it requires? If not, why not?

In column 1, list your clients who will need to be transferred to another employee or partner, and the person designated to take over responsibility for each of these clients when you leave. Have you started to groom those successors for their role? In the second column, indicate what you are doing to prepare your successors and facilitate the client transition. In the third column, list how long you estimate this will take.

Client and Successor	Actions Being Taken	How Long?

For each client relationship where your successor has not yet been identified, fill in the chart below. Indicate the possible successors for each client, and the pros and cons for each candidate, including the factors that will help you decide their suitability and readiness. In the last column, indicate any other individuals who should be involved in the selection process (e.g., the client).

Client	Possible Successors	Pros/Cons	Others to Involve

Client	Possible Successors	Pros/Cons	Others to Involve

Once you select the successor for the client relationship, complete the chart below. List the client and successor, indicate what needs to be done by you and others to prepare the successor for that role, and state when you will begin the client transition process.

Client and Successor	What Needs to Be Done to Prepare Successor	Start Date

What worries do you have about transitioning your clients to another person?

____

____

____

What can you do to allay those concerns?

____

____

____

Have you spoken with your clients about your future plans and the eventual transfer of client responsibility to other people in your firm?

❑ Yes ❑ No *If no, when will you do it?* ________________________

____

What questions, concerns, or objections do you anticipate the clients may have? How will you address them?

____

____

____

Are there any partners, managers, administrators, or staff who should be informed about your client transition plans, and if so, have you told them?

Name: ______________________________ told? ❑ Yes ❑ No

Name: ______________________________ told? ❑ Yes ❑ No

Name: ______________________________ told? ❑ Yes ❑ No

Name: ______________________________ told? ❑ Yes ❑ No

Name: ______________________________ told? ❑ Yes ❑ No

If you have not told any partners, managers, administrators, or staff about your client transition plans, when will you do it?

____

____

____

What questions, concerns, or objections do you anticipate your partners, managers, administrators, or staff may have and how will you address them?

______

______

______

Outline Your Terms for Retirement

Whether you are an owner, partner, or employee, outline a plan for retiring from the firm or company that lays out the terms on which you would like to retire. After you draft your plan, consider the following questions:

- How do you think the company, your partners, and your colleagues will respond to your plan?
- Will your plan address both your needs and theirs?
- If your needs and theirs will differ, is there a way to bridge the gaps?

______

______

______

______

Respond to Requests

After you retire, clients, friends, and family members may continue to ask you for professional help or favors. You may feel torn between wanting to help them and wanting to give up this work. Think about how you will respond to such requests. Write down two or three possible responses.

1. ______
2. ______
3. ______

 Visualize the Reaction You Desire

Sometimes, you may avoid bringing up your plans or thoughts about retirement at work or at home because you are concerned people will react negatively. But imagining a positive outcome can motivate you to do it. This exercise will help you present your ideas about retirement to someone in a way that is more likely to elicit a positive response from them. To make this happen, you will pretend that you have *already* had a successful conversation about retirement, then think about what you will do to make that positive outcome a reality.

Relax. Sit comfortably, away from distractions, including phones and computers.

Begin with the subject of the conversation. What is the message you want to convey? Who is the intended recipient?

Close your eyes and visualize yourself giving the person your message. Now, visualize that the other person is smiling and happy to hear what you say. Listen as they voice their support. That positive response is your goal.

How do you feel when you see the other person smile and when you hear their support?

____

____

____

What aspects of your message is the person especially pleased with?

____

____

____

Remember the person's happy face and keep it in mind as you open your eyes and answer the following questions. In order for your actual conversation to produce this positive response:

How will you lay the groundwork for the actual conversation?

____

____

How and what will you prepare in advance?

How will you start the conversation?

What points will you emphasize?

What tone of voice will you use?

What will make the timing right?

What will make the environment right?

What else will you do to make the conversation successful?

When you review your answers, you will have a blueprint for what to do to achieve the positive outcome you visualized in your imagination.

Chapter Review

1. What have you learned about yourself in this chapter? List your five most important insights.

1. ____

2. ____

3. ____

4. ____

5. ____

2. What do your insights suggest about your choices for your future retirement?

3. List three to five decisions you have made or are considering about your retirement after completing this chapter.

1. ____

2. ____

3. ____

4. ____

5. ____

Additional Notes and Action Items

Use this space to record additional notes or observations, as well any action items they inspire.

CHAPTER 5

KNOWING WHO YOU ARE AND HOW YOU GOT HERE

> We go through life. We shed our skins. We become ourselves.
>
> —PATTI SMITH

Self-awareness is critical when you are making decisions about your future. Many professionals restrain their innermost desires and aspirations during their careers in order to meet the expectations of others and perform their professional duties. Retirement is your chance to be the most "authentic" you possible.

The first part of this chapter looks at the "current you." The questions and exercises will help you look inward at the person you are and the values you hold dear. You will examine your strongest abilities, talents, and skills. Don't rush through it. Don't judge yourself. Take time to think deeply about the person you are and the things that are important to you.

This chapter also examines how you think and what you feel about work. After a long career where work has defined a large part of who you are, it is important to understand the role of "work"—however you define it—in your identity, your life up to now, and your future.

The chapter exercises will give you the chance to take a close look at how you spend your time now, how satisfied you are with your current life, and how you would like to spend your time when you have the freedom to choose what will fill your hours every day.

Lastly, this chapter will guide you in taking an overview of your life to date and the significant events and experiences that have formed you. Reflecting on what has shaped you up to this point will help you decide how you want to live your life in the future. It will help you understand how your past has contributed to your strengths and set you up to move forward with self-determination.

What Matters Most to You?

As you reflect on the questions in this chapter, it might be helpful to consider a distinction made by author David Brooks. Brooks distinguishes between "résumé virtues" and "eulogy virtues." He defines résumé virtues as the abilities and achievements that lead to success in the marketplace—things like hard work, association with prestigious schools and firms, leadership skills, and professional accomplishments. Eulogy virtues are those you want to be remembered for, "the ones that are talked about at your funeral," and which lead to a life well-lived. They focus on your inner character, on such traits as kindness, compassion, humility, integrity, courage, or service to others. Retirement can be a time to assess—and if necessary, adjust—the priority of résumé and eulogy virtues in your life.

THE "CURRENT YOU"

The following questions are intended to provoke you to think about your values, your drives, and your legacy. Take your time; these questions require serious introspection. Return to them from time to time and think about them some more. Your answers will affect the decisions you make as you create your future.

Who Are You?

List 10 words that you would use to describe yourself.

1. ______________________ 6. ______________________

2. ______________________ 7. ______________________

3. ______________________ 8. ______________________

4. ______________________ 9. ______________________

5. ______________________ 10. ______________________

Are you happy with your list?

❑ Yes ❑ No

Are there any qualities on your list you would like to drop? What are they and what would you like to replace them with?

What can you do to make each new "replacement" quality an accurate description of yourself?

Identify Your Strengths

What are your greatest strengths, including your talents, skills, knowledge, experience, and personal attributes? List as many as you can.

How have you utilized your strengths in the past?

How are you able to utilize these strengths now?

Are there strengths you are not currently using?

What Is Important to You?

What gives your life meaning?

What do you love to do?

What are you passionate about?

Do you feel you have a purpose or calling in life? What is it?

What drives you? Motivates you? Makes you excited to get up in the morning?

____

____

____

Are you involved in any charitable, political, religious, or other causes that are important to you? Why are they important to you?

____

____

____

What do you want to be remembered for? What would you like your legacy to be?

____

____

____

What kind of impact do you want to have on the world? What have you done until now to achieve it? What do you want your future impact to be?

____

____

____

If you look back 20 years from now, what will make you feel you have led a full and meaningful life?

____

____

____

 Identify Your Most Important Values

Values are the things you believe are most important in the way you lead your life. They are the principles you stand for. When you live your life in sync with your values, you feel steady and on course. When your values are not expressed in what you do every day, it may be unsettling. The following exercises will help you become more aware of your values. As you design your retirement, this self-awareness can help you align your future life with your values

Circle the values below that are important to you. Choose as many as you like. If you hold values that are not on the list, add them at the end.

Achievement	Faith	Pleasure
Adventure	Friendship	Power
Authenticity	Harmony	Respect
Autonomy	Independence	Security
Challenge	Innovation	Service
Collaboration	Integrity	Trustworthiness
Compassion	Joyfulness	Truthfulness
Connection	Justice	Vitality
Control	Kindness	Wealth
Creativity	Knowledge	Wisdom
Decisiveness	Leadership	Other: ____________
Efficiency	Loyalty	Other: ____________
Excitement	Mastery	Other: ____________
Expertise	Order	Other: ____________

Complete the following in the table below:

List your top 5 values in the "Value" column. For each value, explain what it means to you and why it's important. Now think of a time in your life when that value was honored; describe what that felt like. Finally, rank your values in order of importance, by writing the importance number to the left of the value box.

Rank	Value	Why it's important	What it felt like

Indicate below whether you are honoring your top five values in your life right now.

Value__________________ being honored now? ❑ Yes ❑ Yes, but not enough ❑ No

Value__________________ being honored now? ❑ Yes ❑ Yes, but not enough ❑ No

Value__________________ being honored now? ❑ Yes ❑ Yes, but not enough ❑ No

Value__________________ being honored now? ❑ Yes ❑ Yes, but not enough ❑ No

Value__________________ being honored now? ❑ Yes ❑ Yes, but not enough ❑ No

What will you do to ensure that your top five values are regularly honored in the future?

 Examine Your Attitudes about Work

Work has played a central role in your life for a very long time, but have you thought about what work actually means to you? The values you associate with work will influence what you choose to do in retirement. Your frame of mind will be different if your work has been a source of deep meaning and inspiration than if you have worked primarily for a paycheck. If your work has defined who you are, you will be in a different place mentally and emotionally than if it has been just a job. Answer the questions below to help you recognize how you feel about work, so you can design a more meaningful retirement.

What does work mean to you? How do you feel about work?

____

____

____

Why do you work?

____

____

____

Aside from financial rewards, how have you benefited from work? For example, does it give you personal fulfillment, are you providing a valuable service to others, or have you met interesting people?

____

____

____

How important is work to your sense of who you are?

____

____

____

How important is it to you to keep working? Circle where you fall on the scale below (1 = extremely important, I can't imagine my life without work; 5 = Important because it gives me meaning and enjoyment; and 10 = I'll be fine if I stop working).

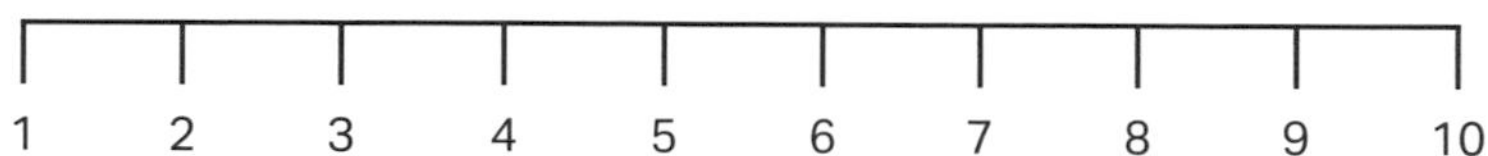

What kind of work do you consider worthwhile?

____

____

____

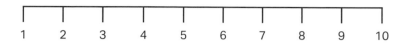

Examine Your Spirituality

Many people find that retirement is a time for seeking greater understanding about the meaning of life. Retirement raises questions about aging, mortality, and an unknown future. As the activities of building a career and raising a family wind down, it is natural to spend more time looking inward and reflecting on life's bigger questions. In the context of planning for retirement, spirituality refers to a search for self-identity and a sense of purpose. Religion is a large part of life for many people when they retire, but the idea of spirituality is broader than organized religion. Designing your retirement offers a time to think deeply about this aspect of your life and what, if any, role it will play in your future.

How important is religion or spirituality to you?

____

____

____

Are you a member of a church, synagogue, mosque, or other religious community?

____

____

____

Do you practice a faith or spiritual tradition and, if so, how will it affect your choices in retirement?

Would you like to explore a faith or spiritual tradition? Would it be out of intellectual interest, for a greater sense of purpose, or for another reason?

Do you have a deep spiritual sense of living your life for a purpose and, if so, what is it?

Is it spiritually important to you to give to others in some way? How might you do that in your retirement plans?

WHERE YOUR TIME GOES

How Do You Spend Your Time Now?

Your life in the future is likely to be considerably different from how it is now. The time you now allocate to work, for example, may diminish, while the time you devote to grandchildren, leisure activities, or personal health and fitness may increase. Even if you are constrained due to financial, family, or other pressures, you have freedom to make your own choices. This exercise will help you examine how you spend your time now and how much enjoyment those activities bring you.

In the circle below, create a pie chart that shows how you spend your time now. Divide the circle into sections, with each slice representing the portion of time you devote *each week* to these general categories:

1. Work
2. Home and Family
3. Fun and Recreation
4. Self
5. Community
6. Other

Then, in each slice, list the activities that occupy your time.

- In "Self," include sleep, exercise, friendships, personal development, private time, spiritual practice, and creative expression.
- In "Community," include socializing, civic and political involvement, volunteer work, and charitable activities.

How You Spend Your Time Now

Referring to your pie chart, how would you rate the time and attention you currently spend in the areas listed below? Check off whether you spend too little, the right amount, or too much time in each area.

Area of Life	Too little	Just right	Too much
Self			
Home and family			
Work			
Leisure			
Volunteering			
Fun and recreation			
Community involvement			
Political activities			
Travel for work			
Travel for enjoyment			
Adventure			
Exercise and health			
Friendships			
Spiritual practice			
Learning			
Cultural activities			
Creative expression			
Hobbies			
Private time			
Socializing			
Charitable activities			
Other			

In terms of the time and energy you spend in these areas,

Which are you happiest with?

Which do you find meaningful?

Which do you want to do more of?

Which do you want to do less of?

What areas would you like to add?

How Satisfied Are You with How You Spend Your Time?

How satisfied are you with the time you devote to each of the areas listed below? Check the box that best represents your feelings for each area. At the bottom, add up the checkmarks in each column.

Area of Life	Satisfied	Neutral	Dissatisfied
Spouse/Partner			
Family			
Work			
Health and Well-being			
Friendships			
Obligations to others			
Fun/Recreation			
Learning and Personal Growth			
Creative Pursuits			
Spiritual Life			
Degree of Autonomy			
Personal Development			
Social Life			
Time Management			
Leisure Travel			
Contributing to Society			
Physical Environment			
TOTAL			

If you checked "satisfied" for most of your answers, you're a happy camper!

For the areas where you are "neutral" or "dissatisfied," what can you do to increase your satisfaction level?

If many of your answers fall into the "dissatisfied" column, it's time to make some serious changes. For each area of dissatisfaction, begin to identify specific steps you can take to turn it around. Consider whether it might be helpful to get some professional counseling.

How Do You Want to Spend Your Time in the Future?

Now that you have closely examined how you currently spend your time, think about how you want to spend your time in the future.

Create a second pie chart. Divide the circle into sections again, but this time make the slices represent the portion of time you want to devote *each week* to these categories (or to new categories that you choose) in the future:

Then, in each slice, list the activities that will occupy your time.

1. Work
2. Home and Family
3. Fun and Recreation
4. Self
5. Community
6. Other

How Do You Want to Spend Your Time in the Future?

REFLECTING ON YOUR LIFE

As we age and especially when we have the unstructured time that retirement can afford, we can go on a journey of self-discovery. By learning not just who we have become, but also what influences shaped us and how our past choices and experiences affected us, we can make wiser choices about our future. We can also become more resilient. Understanding how we dealt successfully with problems in the past enables us to remain positive in the face of future challenges and setbacks, and to deal better with unexpected events.

Below are two alternative reflective exercises, one narrative (an autobiography) and the other visual (an autobiographical timeline). Complete one or both of them.

Your Autobiography

Write your autobiography, highlighting key events and experiences, both positive and negative. You can outline the key points here and use extra pages for more details.

 Your Autobiographical Timeline

Fill in the timeline below, listing significant life events, influences, and experiences during each decade.

TIMELINE OF SIGNIFICANT EVENTS AND EXPERIENCES IN YOUR LIFE

Age	Positive Events	Negative Events
Birth		
10		
20		
30		
40		
50		
60		
70+		

Examine Your Significant Transitions

Some of the significant events you wrote about in your autobiography or noted on your timeline likely involved significant transitions. As you now embark on another major transition, think about how you managed the earlier ones.

What do you recall about how you felt during the transition process?

What was especially helpful to you during the transition?

Did anything make the transition especially difficult? How did you deal with it?

Who helped you navigate the transition process?

As you reflect on previous transitions, do you see any repeated themes or patterns? How can you use what you see to ease your current transition?

Reflect on Your Autobiography or Timeline

What were the three to five best experiences in your life and what made them so good?

What did you learn from them?

What were the three to five worst things that happened in your life and what made them so awful?

What did you learn about yourself from them?

Who/what were the most important influences in your life and in what way(s) did they affect you?

What values have you tried to uphold in your life and which experiences reflect those values?

What were the best decisions you made in your life?

What decisions do you wish you had made differently?

Do you have any regrets in any aspects of your life? What are they?

What do you wish you had done more of/less of/differently?

Do any relationships, experiences, or failures remain unresolved and, if so, are they preventing you from moving forward?

If you have unresolved issues, what would help you resolve them?

Did you once have any dreams or aspirations that remain unfulfilled and, if so, what factors prevented you from fulfilling those dreams?

Could you fulfill them now and, if so, how would you do it?

Reflect on Your Youthful Goals

Think about when you were young. What kind of life did you expect to have? What were your life goals?

How does your current life conform to or differ from what you expected?

Did you achieve your life goals?

How do your answers to these questions make you feel?

Examine Your Comfort Level with Taking Risks

What kind of risk-taker are you? Circle the category that applies.

Risk-Seeking

Adventurous

Bold

Moderate

Cautious

Risk-averse

What were the most significant risks you took in your life and how did they turn out?

How did they affect your willingness to take other risks?

What did you learn about yourself as a risk-taker?

What do you consider the biggest risks you may have to take in this new stage of your life?

How do you feel about taking those risks?

Mark where your answer falls on this scale (1 = exhilarated and 10 = terrified).

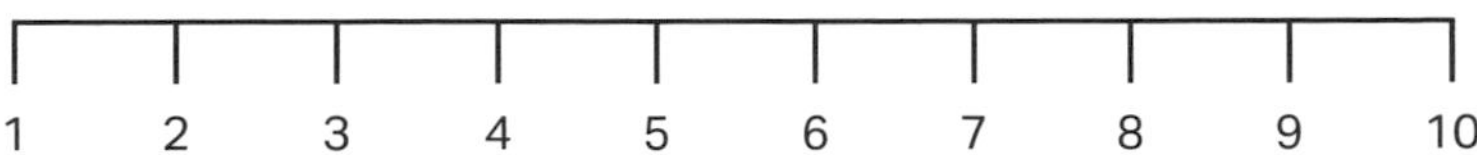

Will your fear of those risks prevent you from creating the retirement you would like?

____

____

____

What can you do to reduce the risks you anticipate?

____

____

____

What else can you do to make yourself more comfortable about taking those risks?

____

____

____

Reflect on Significant Past Situations

When trying to decide how you want to spend your time in the future, it may be helpful to consider how you behaved and felt in various situations in the past. The following questions, which ask you to complete a sentence, are designed to help you discern what kinds of activities and environments you want to look for—or avoid—as you make your plans for retirement. In answering these questions, do not limit yourself to work but consider all situations, past and present, including home and family, community and charitable activities, hobbies, recreation, and artistic pursuits.

Complete the sentences below. The follow-up questions ask you for details about the situation. List as many specific factors about the situation as possible, including:

- the physical environment
- the people involved
- the reasons you were doing what you were doing
- the stakes involved
- your expectations and those of others
- what you were feeling or experiencing at the time

I was at my best when:____________________

What was it about the situation that made you feel that way?

I felt happiest when:____________________

What was it about the situation that made you feel so happy?

I felt most energized/exhilarated when: ____________________

What was it about the situation that made you feel that way?

I felt the most inspired when: ____________________

What was it about the situation that inspired you?

____

____

____

List three to five past and current activities, events, or pursuits that frustrate you.

1. ____
2. ____
3. ____
4. ____
5. ____

What makes these things so frustrating? List as many specific factors as possible.

____

____

____

____

____

List three to five past and current activities, events, or pursuits that filled you with stress and anxiety.

1. ____
2. ____
3. ____
4. ____
5. ____

What makes you anxious about them? List as many specific factors as possible.

____

____

____

____

____

List three to five past and current activities that take too much out of you.

1. _______________
2. _______________
3. _______________
4. _______________
5. _______________

What makes them so draining? List as many specific factors as possible.

____

____

____

____

____

Reflect on Your Work History

Analyzing the features you liked most and least about your past jobs can help you decide what you will do when you retire, whether that involves a paying job, volunteer work, or any organized activities. Most likely, some jobs were more enjoyable, fulfilling, and rewarding than others. You might have had jobs that brought you joy and others that you couldn't wait to leave.

List the various jobs and positions you have held and places you have worked. Include paid and volunteer jobs.

Which jobs and positions were your favorites? Why? List as many reasons as you can.

Which jobs and positions did you like least? Why? List as many reasons as you can.

What were the key lessons you learned in each job or position? Include lessons about life generally, about your profession, or about yourself, including your preferences, needs, strengths, and values.

YOUR FAVORITE SKILLS AND INTERESTS

Over the years you have developed various skills and interests. Closely examining your favorite skills and interests will increase your awareness of what you enjoy and would like to do when you retire. Retirement is a time to expand your thinking and embrace all the abilities and interests you enjoy, not just the ones you have focused on during your working life. Many people think they can only use their skills in the same ways they have in the past. Analyzing your skills more carefully can help you realize you have more options than you think to apply your talents in new ways. Retirement affords you the time to pursue the ones you care about most. When you understand your skills and interests in greater depth, you can be more creative about how to make them part of your retirement.

Skills and Interests You Developed through Paid and Unpaid Work

In column one of the first chart below, list work you have done for pay. In the second chart, list your major unpaid endeavors, such as hobbies, volunteering, and playing a musical instrument. In both charts, go as far back as high school. Then, use the second column in both charts to describe your activities and skills in those roles. In the third column, indicate the key features that you liked most about the job or activity. Sample entries are provided to give you ideas for filling in the charts.

CHART 1: PAID WORK

Paid Jobs	Activities/Skills	Favorite Features
Waiter	Serving, customer service	Learning about food and meals, helping customers
Administrative assistant, medical training program	Organizing, program planning, program administration, dealing with house staff	Focus on family medicine, dealing with intelligent and dedicated people, always learning new things, community focus

CHART 1: PAID WORK

Paid Jobs	Activities/Skills	Favorite Features

CHART 2: UNPAID WORK

Unpaid Endeavors	Activities/Skills	Favorite Features
Board Member, nonprofit	Strategic planning, overseeing agency management, financial planning, fundraising	Serving children and families in need, being a leader, setting the future course of the agency
Book club	Reading, organizing and maintaining group, researching books	Reading a variety of books, meeting with friends, stimulating discussions, learning new things

Take a careful look at what you entered in both charts and circle the words in the second and third columns that still appeal to you today. Which would you like to continue in the future? Do you see any patterns or items that recur in different contexts? List those activities, skills, and features that you most favor in the first column of Chart 3 below.

In the second column of Chart 3, write down some ideas for how you might include those items in the activities you pursue going forward. Consider how you might combine skills and interests in different ways. For example, if you have leadership skills and also enjoy the outdoors, you might become a wilderness guide; if you have mediation skills, you might teach conflict resolution to grade school students.

CHART 3

Activities/Skills	How to Include in the Future

WHAT YOU THINK ABOUT YOUR LIFE SO FAR

This chapter has asked you to look deeply into yourself and examine the things that matter most to you and those that have most affected you. The questions have explored many aspects of your life, past and current. Below are some questions to help you bring your thoughts together and reflect on what they mean for your future.

How pleased are you with your life, overall?

What do you love most about your life?

In what areas are you most satisfied?

In what areas are you most disappointed?

What about your life would you like to change?

What's missing from your life that you would like to add?

What are your greatest accomplishments?

What have been the driving forces in your life? Have they changed over time?

Chapter Review

1. *This chapter has asked you to examine your life in the past and the present. When you retire, many things in your life will change. List the major changes you anticipate and describe how your life up to now has prepared you to deal with those changes in the future.*

2. *What have you learned about yourself in this chapter? List your five most important insights.*

1. ______________________________

2. ______________________________

3. ______________________________

4. ______________________________

5. ______________________________

3. *What do your insights suggest about your choices for your future retirement?*

____

____

____

4. *List three to five decisions you have made or are considering about your retirement after completing this chapter.*

1. ______________________________

2. ______________________________

3. ______________________________

4. ______________________________

5. ______________________________

 Additional Notes and Action Items

Use this space to record additional notes or observations, as well any action items they inspire.

CHAPTER 6

THE IMPACT OF RETIREMENT ON YOUR RELATIONSHIPS

> Call it a clan, call it a network, call it a tribe, call it a family: Whatever you call it, whoever you are, you need one.
>
> —JANE HOWARD

The decisions you make and the actions you take regarding your retirement will impact not just you but also those close to you, such as your spouse or partner and other members of your family. It is important to take them into account as you go through this transition. It is also important to think about how retirement will affect your relationships with friends and acquaintances so that you maintain social connections when your career status changes and time goes on.

The exercises that appear in the first part of this chapter will help you think about which family members you should consider in planning for retirement and what they may need and expect from you when you retire. The exercises present specific questions about how your retirement will affect your spouse or life partner, children, grandchildren, parents, siblings, and other relatives. The second part of the chapter deals with friends and social relationships. The exercises in that part of the chapter will help you consider how to preserve existing friendships and relationships, build new ones in the future, and remain socially engaged when you retire.

YOUR SPOUSE/LIFE PARTNER

People expect that retirement will allow them to enjoy more pleasure and less stress with their spouse. For many, this is the case. But problems often arise when spouses have their own assumptions about what retirement will be like, and those assumptions are not in sync or clearly communicated. In fact, the US divorce rate has declined since the 1990s for all age groups except people aged 50 and older. For that group, the divorce rate has *doubled;* for those aged 65 and up, the rate has *tripled*. (This phenomenon has been labeled "gray divorce.") Much of the discontent behind this increase is due to disconnections and tensions that surface in retirement.

Retirement transitions involve significant changes and difficult adjustments for both spouses. Disagreements about major issues, such as how to spend the retirement budget, can cause outright conflicts. But even seemingly small things, like who will shop for groceries or plan social activities, can become points of contention. Differences about how much time you'll spend together and apart every day, and what you each will do during those times, can be particularly challenging for a marital relationship when one or both spouses retire. That's why identifying each spouse's priorities, attitudes, and expectations about retirement and each other is critically important. The earlier and more regularly you discuss assumptions and feelings, negotiate and resolve differences, and create mutually agreeable plans, the more likely it is that you will enjoy a happy and harmonious retirement as a couple.

Examine Your Relationship

In the following exercise, circle the answer that most closely reflects your relationship with your spouse/partner.

My relationship with my spouse/partner is:

❑ Excellent ❑ Good ❑ Problematic

We discuss our future plans together:

❑ Regularly ❑ Sometimes ❑ Rarely

Regarding our plans for the future, we agree on:

❑ Most things ❑ Some things ❑ Few things ❑ I don't know

Regarding our expectations for each other in the future, we are:

❑ In agreement ❑ Still working it out ❑ Uncertain ❑ In disagreement ❑ I don't know

Who is retiring?

❏ Just me—my spouse already retired or has not been employed.

❏ Just me—my spouse will continue working for another ____ months/years.

❏ Just my spouse.

❏ We are both retiring at about the same time.

If one of you keeps working and the other retires,

...how will it affect your respective household roles and responsibilities?

____

____

____

...how will it affect the retired spouse's desires for life in retirement (for example, if the retired spouse wants to travel more)?

____

____

____

...what adjustments will you have to make?

____

____

____

Have you discussed these issues with your spouse? If not, when will you have that discussion?

Home-Based Spouses

Some people are "home-based" because they work from a home office, are a homemaker, have not held an outside job, or have already retired. The following questions encourage you to think about how your retirement may affect the daily routine of your home-based spouse, or how they may affect you if you work at home.

If you are not accustomed to being together all day every day, how much "togetherness" do you want and expect from your home-based spouse?

Will you be independent, active, and out of the house much of the time? Or will you expect your home-based spouse to be available at home and attentive to your needs?

To what extent will your presence at home interfere with your spouse's usual schedule? If your spouse works from home, will your presence interrupt the privacy she/he needs and is used to?

____

____

____

If you plan to work in some capacity from home, will there be adequate space and privacy for both of you?

❏ Yes ❏ No

If you are home-based and your retiring spouse has been working outside the home, how will his/her retirement affect your daily routine?

____

____

____

____

If You Are Both Retiring

How will it affect your respective household roles and responsibilities?

____

____

____

____

How much "togetherness" does each of you want and expect?

How much independence does each of you want and expect in your daily lives?

Examine Your Shared Interests and Activities

What hobbies and activities does each of you enjoy?

You

Spouse

When you retire, which of these hobbies and activities will you do together and which separately?

____

____

____

____

Shared Interests and Activities

If you will both be retired, think about interests you share with your spouse and some activities you might do together. Here are a few ideas:

- Travel and study abroad
- Travel and work abroad
- Take classes together
- Become docents at local museums, landmarks, historical sites, cultural sites, conservation areas, zoos, botanical gardens, or other places that interest you
- Get involved in political activities and campaigns
- Volunteer for the same organization
- Work with children
- Start a nonprofit that benefits a cause or group you care about
- Open a business together (see Starting a New Business on page 182 for some examples)

How many fixed commitments such as board positions or volunteer obligations will each of you continue or accept?

____

____

____

____

How will you accommodate each other's interests, activities, and commitments?

Do you and your spouse each have friends you like to socialize with individually?

Do you like socializing with each other's friends?

How will you decide on and coordinate joint social engagements?

How Will Your Retirement Impact Your Spouse/Life Partner?

What worries you most about the impact of your retirement on your spouse, and how are you addressing those concerns?

____

____

____

How does your spouse feel about your retiring? Check the answers that apply.

- ❑ Excited and happy I'm retiring
- ❑ Wants me to wait longer than I want
- ❑ Is ambivalent
- ❑ Doesn't want me to retire
- ❑ Doesn't care
- ❑ Doesn't know yet
- ❑ I don't know

What is your spouse most concerned about, and how are you addressing those concerns?

____

____

____

Has your spouse told you of those feelings and concerns or are you assuming them?

____

____

____

 Discussions with Your Spouse/Life Partner

Have you discussed the issues and expectations suggested by the questions in this Chapter with your spouse? If not:

What reactions do you expect from your spouse?

____

____

Are you concerned about any of those reactions?

____

____

When will you have the conversation? Give yourself a deadline: ______________

What will you do to prepare for it?

____

____

If your answers to any of the foregoing questions reveal possible conflicts, what can be done to prevent or resolve them?

____

____

____

 Brainwrite with Your Spouse or Partner

"Brainwriting," like brainstorming, is a group process for generating ideas and solutions to problems. But unlike brainstorming, where group members vocalize ideas at the same time, brainwriting is first done alone. Individual members generate their own list of ideas privately, then the group reviews them all together.

In this exercise:

- You and your spouse/partner will each spend three to five minutes every day for one week quickly writing down your ideas, concerns, and wishes for retirement.
- At the end of the week, share with each other what you have written.
- Build on each other's ideas and generate new ones triggered by your discussion.
- Decide which ideas would be best, which concerns need to be addressed, and which wishes you want to make come true, and note them below.

PREPARING FOR CHALLENGING DISCUSSIONS

If you want to discuss a subject with your spouse and anticipate some disagreement, it is good to prepare in advance so that you can present your points in a more persuasive and conciliatory way. The chart below will help you think about what is important to you and to your spouse. You can then consider in advance how to address your spouse's interests, needs, and concerns, and frame your position in a more productive way.

Negotiation

You can use the following chart by yourself to organize your thoughts and prepare for a discussion with your spouse. Alternatively, you can make a copy of the chart for your spouse and do the exercise together. You and your spouse can each fill out a chart separately and then discuss your answers together.

1. In the "Goals" box below, indicate your goals and what you think your spouse's are. These are the agreements you and your spouse want to reach.

2. "Interests" relate to the values or other factors that underlie your goals. For example, if your goal is to make money, your underlying interests could be "personal security," "help our kids," or "pay for Grandma's long-term care."

3. "Needs" are "must-haves," what you consider nonnegotiable.

4. "Concerns" are worries about the discussion itself or what will happen if you don't agree.

	Goals	Interests	Needs	Concerns
Mine				
Spouse's				

You can also use the exercise "Visualize the Reaction You Desire" in Chapter 4 to prepare for difficult conversations about retirement with your spouse.

CHILDREN AND GRANDCHILDREN

Whatever the relationship is between you and your children and grandchildren, it is important to be clear about how your retirement will impact them and you. Then you can try to maximize your enjoyment as a parent and grandparent going forward.

Having grandchildren can be one of life's great joys. Retirement is often welcomed as a time for grandparents to spend time with grandkids, both for their own pleasure and to help their adult children take care of them. Ideally, the relationship you have with your children and grandchildren is mutually loving and nurturing, and you all enjoy being with each other. Sometimes, however, your desires to spend more time (or less) with them may not agree with their expectations. Also, in many families, retirees find themselves with significant financial and caregiving responsibilities for grandchildren and/or children. They may be paying tuition, paying off their student loans, or providing support when a child is unemployed. Some may have adult children who depend on them for childcare, and some may be raising grandchildren in their own homes.

Contemplating a Move to Be Near Family

Many retired people want to live near their grandchildren so they can spend time with them, help care for them, and be part of their lives as they grow up. They may also want to live close to adult children to provide help and receive it from them if and when it is needed. But we live in a highly mobile society and it is common for families to live far apart. This tempts many people who retire to move closer to their children and grandchildren. As desirable as this is, it is not easy to pick up, leave a familiar community, relocate, and start over again in a new place. It is also risky. Below are some of the factors to consider when contemplating such a move:

- Would your children welcome having you move nearby? As much as you want to help and participate, be sure the feeling is mutual. Not all children want their parents to be close.
- How much help do they want and how much are you willing to give? Although children may be thrilled for your help with the grandkids, boundaries may be necessary so that your child-rearing help does not begin to feel obligatory or constricting.
- What else will you do in your new community? You will need to build a new social network and find activities to keep you busy aside from your family involvement. Otherwise you may run the risk of becoming dependent on your children or grandchildren for your happiness.
- Can you afford the move? Relocation is expensive, especially if you move to an area with a higher cost of living.
- Do your children live in an area that is geographically desirable to you? Does it offer sufficient opportunities for the kind of social, cultural, athletic, and other activities you enjoy?

- Due to work demands, job changes, or new employment opportunities, your children and their families might have to relocate after you move. Some lines of work may require frequent moves. Would you be ready to move again (and possibly again) to be near them?
- Does your spouse also want to make this move? If your spouse is reluctant or opposed to it, this disagreement may lead to considerable conflict.
- If you have children who live in other locations, what will this move mean to them? How will they perceive and react to your decision?

Consider Your Children and Grandchildren Prior to Retirement

If you have children and/or grandchildren, how will your retirement impact them?

___

___

___

Do you have caregiving, financial, or other responsibilities for children or grandchildren and, if so, what are those responsibilities?

___

___

___

Are any children or grandchildren living with you? Will your retirement affect their living arrangements?

___

___

___

What do your children want or expect from you in terms of time and support for themselves and their children? Are their expectations in sync with yours?

How much time do you want to spend with your children and grandchildren and how much time do you think they want to spend with you?

If your children or grandchildren live far away from you, how often do you want to visit them and how often do they want you to visit?

How will expectations or needs of your children and grandchildren impact your plans for the future?

If there is disagreement between you and your children or grandchildren about expectations, how can it be resolved?

YOUR PARENTS

Increasing longevity applies not just to you but to your parents as well. If your parents are active, healthy, and financially independent, you might not consider them in planning your retirement. In fact, because they are living longer, healthier lives, it may be hard to imagine your parents becoming weak, ill or dependent, or requiring care. Yet the fact that people are living into their 80s, 90s, and 100s increases the likelihood that they will develop chronic diseases and related disabilities, and will require assistance. It is now common for people in their 60s and 70s to be caring for parents in their 90s and older. Twenty million people in the US provide care for an aging parent, and 80% of long-term care is provided by families rather than institutions.

If your parents will need financial support as they age, especially if they become ill, that can be a substantial economic burden on the family. Even if your parents have the financial means to pay for care, the responsibility for caregiving, decisions about housing and caregivers, and medical decision-making may one day rest with you and other family members.

Family dynamics, especially among siblings, around issues of parental caregiving can be complicated and emotional. Rather than wait for a crisis to raise the question of supporting and caring for aging or sick parents, it is a good idea to consider what those responsibilities for your parents are now, what they are likely to become over time, and how they will be shared by family members.

Thinking these issues through as you plan your retirement can help you prepare (and possibly prepare your family) for this situation if and when the time comes. It can also free you to make decisions about your retirement plans that account for any current and contingent obligations to your parents.

 Consider Your Parents Prior to Retirement

How will your retirement affect your proximity to, and your interaction and relationship with, your parents?

____

____

____

If you have financial and/or caregiving responsibilities for your parents, how will your retirement affect those responsibilities?

Do you anticipate financial and/or caregiving responsibilities for your parents in the future?

What constraints do these current or anticipated responsibilities place on your retirement plans?

What can you do—and are you willing to do—to mitigate the constraints?

Are there siblings, other relatives, friends, or caregivers who share responsibility (or are willing to do so) for your parents?

Do you feel any conflict between your retirement desires and your responsibilities to your parents and, if so, what would be a satisfactory resolution of the conflict?

Have you investigated agencies, care providers, and other resources that can help you fulfill your responsibilities to your parents?

Who are the people and organizations you can call on for personal support as you deal with these issues?

Other Relatives

Are there siblings or other relatives who will be affected by your retirement and, if so, how will they be affected?

What is the nature of your responsibilities toward them?

How will those responsibilities impact your retirement and what can you do to mitigate the impact?

FRIENDSHIPS AND SOCIAL RELATIONSHIPS

People are social beings; they need regular social interaction. Without making an effort to get out and stay active, retirement can lead to social isolation, a condition that has been linked to higher risks for a variety of physical and mental ailments, including heart disease, weakened immune system, depression, and cognitive decline. In contrast, engaging in meaningful, enjoyable, and productive activities with other people has been shown to increase well-being, improve cognitive function, and even lead to a longer life.

One of the challenges of getting older is maintaining friendships and social relationships. Retirement exacerbates this situation. When some friends retire and others don't, schedules and interests may become harder to mesh. People move, lose touch, and drift apart. Retirement can also physically cut off a source of important social relationships because you no longer regularly see people in the office or interact with clients.

You can minimize the impact of retirement on your friendships and social relationships by planning and taking the initiative to maintain and expand them. Doing that will allow you to transition into retirement without losing the friends you cherish and help you build new relationships for the future.

Examine Your Circle of Friends and Acquaintances

In the circles on the next page, list the friends who mean the most to you in the center, and moving out from there, write in the names of people whose friendship or acquaintance you value.

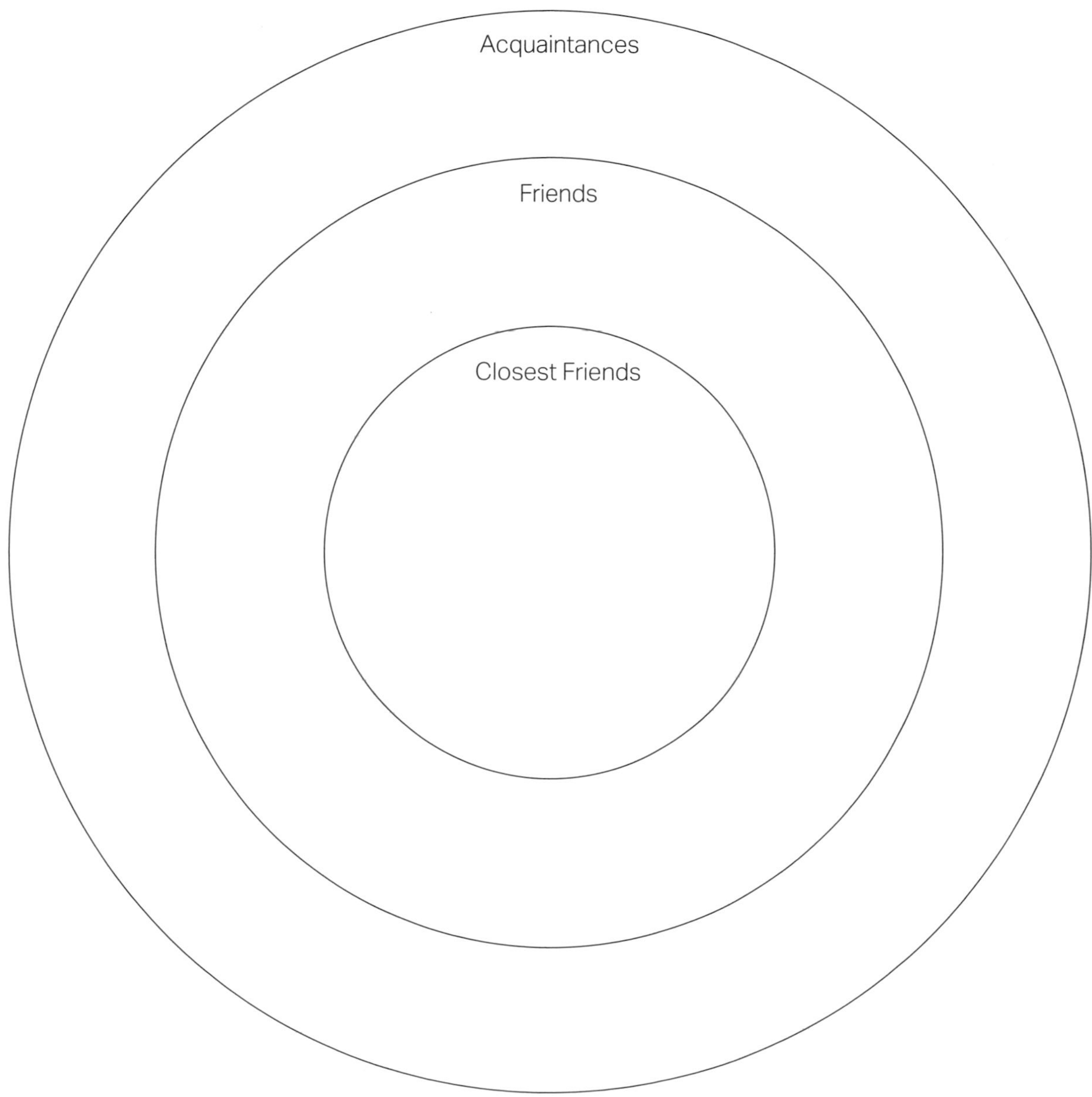

For the people you most want to stay in touch with, note in the box below what you will do to maintain and strengthen those relationships. Be as specific as you can. Indicate what you will do and how frequently you will do it. For example, "I will meet Alex for lunch or coffee once every two weeks."

Friends to Stay in Touch With	Action Item

How is your retirement likely to impact your relationships with your friends?

Which people do you fear losing contact with? What can you do to avoid that?

Which people would you like to know better? What will you do to make that happen?

MAKING NEW FRIENDS

While it's a treasure to enjoy longtime friendships, retirement presents an opportunity—and a need—to make new friends. Connections with friends are vital for good mental, emotional, and physical health, but the number of those connections decline as you get older. Making new friends is hard—but it is essential. You may feel shy, awkward, intimidated, or reluctant to make the effort. But there are many ways and places to meet people who share your interests and are receptive—and even eager—to make new acquaintances and build new friendships.

The Value and Importance of Intergenerational Friendships

Diversifying your social connections is as important as diversifying your financial portfolio. If most of your friends are around the same age as you are, retirement is a time when a conscious effort to cultivate friends from different generations can have significant benefits. Studies have shown that as people get older, having good friends produces more psychological well-being than having good relationships with family members. And having social ties with people who are older and younger is linked with better cognitive functioning and physical and psychological well-being.

Friends whose ages and experiences are different from your own can be enlightening. They can offer different perspectives and ideas from friends your own age. They can constructively challenge you to question your assumptions and habits, consider new possibilities, and think about things in new ways.

Friendships with younger people can introduce you to new activities and experiences that keep your brain agile and your spirit young. They can motivate you to stay active and keep your sense of adventure alive. They can provide hands-on help with tasks along with personal affection. They can also enhance your sense of purpose and enrich your life. Passing along to someone younger the knowledge, wisdom, and skills you have acquired during your lifetime can give you meaning and pleasure. Serving as a mentor, offering care and support along with sage advice, can make you feel valued. More importantly, it is a way to positively impact the lives of younger people.

Similarly, friends who are older can also bring benefits. They can provide insights about life that will serve you as you get older, and help you deal with issues that peers might not understand or be able to help you with. What's more, benefiting them through your companionship and caring will engender their gratitude and make you feel useful, needed, and appreciated.

 How to Meet People after You Retire

List your current activities that bring you into regular contact with people who share similar interests, such as gym classes, religious services, volunteer activities, card playing, or book clubs.

With the activities listed above in mind, note anyone you would like to get to know better and how you would initiate a relationship. For example, would you invite them to join you for coffee or dinner, a movie or a lecture, a walk or a hike?

People to Know Better	How	When

What new activities could you try that would help you meet new people?

1. ________________________
2. ________________________
3. ________________________
4. ________________________
5. ________________________
6. ________________________
7. ________________________
8. ________________________
9. ________________________
10. ________________________

List any solo activities you engage in, such as quilting, coin collecting, or reading that you could turn into a social activity by forming or joining a club or group. Then, write down how you will form or find a group and when you will do it.

Solo Activities	How to Form/Find Group	When

List any former high school, college, or work friends that you would like to reconnect with and how and when you plan to initiate contact. For example, will you be attending an upcoming reunion? Even better, can you join the planning committee?

People to Reconnect With	How	When

Many communities and organizations sponsor events where people can come together around shared interests. Online resources like Meetup.com and Stitch.net also help people find those places and events. After investigating the resources that exist in your community, note the groups you plan to join, when you will join, and what you will do to meet others at the event.

Places or Events to Meet People	Start Date	What You Will Do

If you are single, are you interested in developing a romantic relationship and, if so, what will you do to find a partner? For example, will you join an online dating site or other matching services? Which ones?

____

____

____

What social or other activities might bring you into contact with potential partners?

Do you want friends and family to introduce you to people? If so, note below who you plan to mention this to along with a deadline for doing so.

Online Dating

If you are single, divorced, or widowed in retirement, you may have an interest in dating. Dating at any age can be intimidating, but if you haven't done it for a while, it can be especially daunting. Not only have you changed, physically and emotionally, but the world of dating is completely new. One of the most significant developments is the rise of online dating sites that allow you to find matches who meet the criteria you are looking for in a potential partner. Although you may think these sites are used only by younger people, they are commonly used by people of all ages. A Pew Research study found that between 2013 and 2015, the number of adults aged 55 to 64 who tried online dating doubled, from 6 percent to 12 percent.

Whether you are looking for companionship, a fun date, a lifelong relationship, or an occasional tryst, these sites provide an easy and convenient way to meet people. Some of the sites that are used frequently by people over 50 are: OurTime.com, SilverSingles.com, Stitch.net, SeniorMatch.com, eHarmony.com, and OkCupid.com. Faith-specific sites include JDate.com, ChristianCafe.com, and CatholicMatch.com.

Navigating the world of online dating can be challenging. If you want to give it a try, check out the various resources that are available to guide you through it. Websites and newsletters such as NextAvenue.org, SeniorPlanet.org, and TheSeniorList.com publish articles and columns that deal with dating, intimacy, and sex after 50. Among the topics they cover are comparisons and evaluations of online dating sites, how to open an account and create your online profile, and how to use these sites effectively and safely. In addition, libraries and community centers often host presentations, workshops, and programs on online dating.

Chapter Review

1. *Have you told your family members that you are planning to retire? If not, when and how will you tell them?*

____

____

____

2. *Describe how you will ensure that you and your spouse or partner communicate effectively about your retirement plans.*

____

____

____

3. *Will any of your responsibilities for children, grandchildren, parents, or other family members constrain your retirement options? Describe those constraints.*

____

____

____

4. *List three to five key things you plan to do to enrich your current relationships, including the dates you will do them.*

1. ______________________________
2. ______________________________
3. ______________________________
4. ______________________________
5. ______________________________

5. *What have you learned about yourself and your relationships in this chapter? List your five most important insights.*

1. ______________________________

2. ______________________________

3. ______________________________

4. ______________________________

5. ______________________________

6. *What do your insights suggest about your choices for your future retirement?*

____

____

____

7. *List three to five decisions you have made or are considering about your retirement after completing this chapter.*

1. ______________________________

2. ______________________________

3. ______________________________

4. ______________________________

5. ______________________________

 Additional Notes and Action Items

Use this space to record additional notes or observations, as well any action items they inspire.

CHAPTER 7

POTENTIAL FINANCIAL AND HEALTH CONSTRAINTS

> The bad news is time flies. The good news is you're the pilot.
>
> —MICHAEL ALTSHULER

As you plan for retirement, it is necessary to take the constraints that might limit your choices into account. Future constraints may arise unexpectedly but you know some of them now. And planning with the known constraints in mind will make you better prepared to deal with future surprises when they appear. This chapter will help you recognize and address possible financial constraints as well as limitations related to health.

One of the principal limitations on retirement planning is your anticipated financial status during retirement. For most people, the single greatest retirement fear is outliving your savings and investments. The first part of this chapter poses some basic questions about your financial situation and how you will finance the kind of retirement you want. It will also help you prepare a very basic budget for the first year of your retirement. You will need more than this to plan effectively for the future, but this will at least give you a start if you need it.

Next, you'll examine various nonfinancial factors that may affect the range of your retirement choices, principally your health, fitness, and emotions, but also some of the constraints identified in earlier chapters, such as family responsibilities. It concludes by helping you focus on developing strategies to reduce, manage, or cope with the constraints you identify.

FINANCES AND YOUR RETIREMENT CHOICES

It is critical that you understand your future financial status so that you can plan your activities and lifestyle accordingly. Whether or not you have already done financial planning for retirement, these first few questions below seek to clarify how financially secure you feel about retiring.

Financial Security

How financially secure are you? It's okay to check more than one.

❏ My income during retirement will be sufficient for me to pursue the activities and maintain the lifestyle I desire.

❏ I am worried that my post-retirement income will be insufficient.

❏ I feel secure now but have some concern about whether I will have enough in the future.

❏ I'm not really sure.

❏ Other (describe) ____

____

Indicate on the scale below how well you manage your finances (1 = very well; 3 = moderately well; and 5 = terribly, I need help).

1 2 3 4 5

What do you worry about most regarding your finances for the future?

____

____

____

What are you doing—or could you be doing—to address those concerns?

FINANCIAL PLANNING FOR RETIREMENT

If you do not yet have a fiscal plan for retirement, start to create one right away. Below are some questions to get you started. These are basic questions about your anticipated future income and expenses, and whether the former will be sufficient to cover the latter. With that information, you can develop a retirement budget.

These questions and exercises will help you plan a simple budget for the first few years after you retire. Planning a long-term retirement budget involves many financial uncertainties, such as inflation, taxes, and rates of return on your investments. You will need to consider alternative scenarios that account for these factors and how they will impact your income and expenses over time. Those analyses and calculations will allow you to plan competently and realistically for the long term. For a deeper look into your future financial status and more comprehensive planning, you may want to utilize retirement planning software or retain a financial advisor.

How Do You Plan Your Retirement Finances?

Do you use retirement-planning software to help you plan your retirement finances?

Do you have a financial advisor who helps you plan and manage your finances?

If you do not have a financial advisor, what can you do to obtain the assistance you need? For example, do you have friends or relatives who can recommend an advisor to you? List any ideas that come to mind.

____

____

____

Resources for Financial Planning

You can find many resources to help you calculate, budget, and plan your finances for retirement, many of them at little or no cost. For instance, if you work with a financial firm to manage your 401(k) or IRA account, ask your advisor to run a retirement cash flow projection for you. Many advisors will do this free of charge. In addition, most books and publications on how to plan for retirement focus on financial planning and include forms and guides. And the internet offers resources about every aspect of financial planning for retirement. These resources include websites operated by government agencies, professional associations, organizations for retirees or seniors, and financial management firms. See the Resources section at the end of this workbook for some examples.

Will Your Expected Income Support the Retired Life You Want?

To answer the following questions, you need to know what your income and expenses will be. Here is an easy three-step process to help you analyze your financial needs and whether you will have enough income to support them.

STEP 1: FUTURE INCOME

Map out your anticipated income during retirement. A detailed list of possible sources of income is provided below along with space to note the estimated income you expect to receive from each of them (if applicable to you).

In completing this chart, list the monthly income you will count on during the first year of your retirement. In subsequent years, you can refer to this list and update it, reflecting any changes in sources or amount of expected income. For that reason, you may want to complete the table using a pencil or make and work from a photocopy.

SOURCES OF EXPECTED INCOME FOR: ___________ (year)

Source	Expected Monthly Income
Income from work	
Pensions	
Social security	
IRAs	
Certificates of deposit	
401(k) plans	
Annuities	
Stocks	
Bonds	
Mutual funds	
Rental properties	
Royalties or other intellectual property	
Interest and principal on loans you made	
Ownership interest in private firms or companies	
Return of capital	
Insurance	
Trusts	
Veterans' benefits	
Other:	
Other:	
Other	

total expected MONTHLY income: $_____________

Multiply x 12

expected ANNUAL income : $_____________

STEP 2: FUTURE EXPENSES

How much money will you need when you retire? In completing this chart, estimate your monthly living expenses for your first year of retirement. In subsequent years, you can refer to this list and update it, reflecting any changes in items or amount of anticipated expenses. For that reason, you may want to complete the table using a pencil or make and work from a photocopy.

ESTIMATED EXPENSES FOR: ___________ (year)

Item	Estimated Monthly Expense
Housing (e.g., mortgage, rent)	
Food and toiletries	
Medical care and prescriptions (excluding health insurance)	
Taxes	
Utilities (e.g., gas, electric, oil)	
Telephone (cell and land line)	
Technology, data usage, digital subscriptions	
Home maintenance (e.g., cleaning, gardening, repairs)	
Debts and obligations (e.g., credit cards, spousal/child support)	
Car, gas, and transportation	
Insurance (e.g., health, auto, home)	
Clothing	
Personal products and services (e.g., manicures, haircuts)	
Membership fees (e.g., gym, country club, subscriptions)	
Family care	
Travel and leisure	
Entertainment (e.g., dining out, concerts, sports events)	
Charitable donations	
Other:	
Other:	
Other	

total estimated MONTHLY expenses: $____________

Multiply x 12

estimated ANNUAL expenses: $____________

STEP 3: SUBTRACT YOUR ANNUAL ESTIMATED EXPENSES FOR THE YEAR FROM YOUR ANNUAL EXPECTED INCOME

Estimated Difference Between Income and Expenses________________ (year)

annual expected income: $____________

annual estimated expenses: - $____________

Difference: $____________

Will your anticipated income be sufficient to cover your anticipated expenses, or will there be a shortfall?

____

____

____

Will your future income be sufficient to support the lifestyle you desire? If not, what adjustments and compromises are you willing to make?

____

____

____

Do you have sufficient savings or assets to cover any projected shortfalls?

❑ Yes ❑ No

If this financial picture is indicative of your long-term finances, how will you be able to cover any budgetary deficits without depleting your savings or assets for the future?

____

____

____

How much money will you need to cover any major expenses in the next few years, such as significant home repairs, moving to another location, or starting a new business? How will those expenses impact your retirement budget?

Do you have a plan to cover unexpected medical needs and long-term health care? For example, what resources and assets would you use to pay for any uncovered medical costs? How much will your current insurance cover?

Highlight Your Expenditures

Gather your electronic and paper credit card and bank account statements for the last 6 to 12 months. Using different colored markers or pens, highlight your expenditures by these categories:

- Essentials (e.g., food, housing, health care)
- Nonessential monthly expenses (e.g., subscriptions, house cleaner, club memberships)
- Required non-monthly expenses (e.g., insurance premiums, property taxes, utilities paid quarterly)
- Discretionary expenses (e.g., entertainment, travel, concerts, hobbies, sports)

What did this exercise tell you about how you are spending your money—and what, if anything, you need to change?

If the estimated income and expenses for your first year of retirement that you calculated above showed a shortfall, identify areas where you can reduce your expenses or make other adjustments to reach a balanced budget.

Live on Your Retirement Budget

Spend one month living on your retirement budget. At the end of the month, evaluate how easy or hard it was and whether you want or need to make any adjustments.

HEALTH AND WELL-BEING: FACTORS THAT MAY AFFECT YOUR RETIREMENT CHOICES

In contemplating future options, your choices may be affected by various factors other than finances. Aside from financial limitations, your overall health, both physical and mental, will have the greatest impact on the activities you can enjoy when you retire. The following exercises are designed to help you think about those issues now so you can prepare for a healthy and fit retirement.

 Health and Fitness

On a scale of 1 to 10, with 1 being "Very poor" and 10 being "Excellent," how would you rate the current status of your:

Physical health: ____________ Physical fitness: ____________ Mental health: ____________

Do you have any current physical or emotional problems that will limit your options in retirement?

____

____

____

Do you have any worries about future health problems that will limit your options in retirement?

____

____

____

When did you last have a physical checkup with your doctor? If you have not had one recently, when do you plan to have one?

____

____

____

If you recently had an annual physical exam, what did your doctor tell you about your health? Did the doctor recommend any changes and, if so, have you made those changes?

____

____

____

If you are in good health, what will you do to maintain your health?

If you are not pleased with the state of your health, what will you do to improve it? If you are not sure what to do, how can you find out?

Do you have the discipline to follow through on any plans you make to improve your health and, if not, what can you do to make yourself more disciplined?

What guidance, support, and resources will you need to improve your health?

Check the most accurate answers:

1. *Do you follow a healthy lifestyle?*

❏ Always ❏ Most of the time ❏ Occasionally ❏ Hardly ever ❏ Never

2. *Do you maintain good eating habits?*

❏ Always ❏ Most of the time ❏ Occasionally ❏ Hardly ever ❏ Never

3. *Do you get sufficient sleep (usually seven to eight hours a night)?*

❑ Always ❑ Most of the time ❑ Occasionally ❑ Hardly ever ❑ Never

4. How much stamina and energy do you have?

❑ Plenty ❑ Enough ❑ Not as much as I need ❑ Very little

If your answers to questions 1 to 3 are not "always" or "most of the time," and if your answer to question 4 is not "plenty" or "enough," it is time to pay closer attention to your health and perhaps visit your doctor.

The Importance of Exercise

It is vitally important to stay physically active when you retire. After a busy, sometimes exhausting, career, it can be tempting to just relax and do nothing. That's fine for a short time, but being sedentary and inactive can lead to increased risk of diabetes, heart attack, stroke, cognitive decline, and depression. It is critical for your health and well-being to keep your body moving. Exercise increases your strength and resilience, and helps prevent and reduce the impact of illness and chronic disease. It also keeps your mind sharp and benefits mental health by reducing anxiety, improving mood and self-confidence, improving sleep, and preventing boredom and loneliness. And it boosts your energy so that you can enjoy your retirement activities.

If you haven't already established an exercise routine, now is the time to start. Focus on building endurance, strength, balance, and flexibility. You do not have to run marathons or climb mountains. Your activities can be as simple as walking, gardening, swimming, or dancing. You can hire a trainer; join a pool, gym, or fitness center; find a walking, hiking, or bicycling club; set a regular golf date with friends; or take group exercise classes at a local community center. (See if you qualify for a discounted membership at your local gym or health center or through your health plan.) The important thing is to exercise regularly and consistently. Build it into your schedule as you design your life in retirement.

 Do You Exercise Regularly?

Describe your exercise routine.

When you retire, do you want to change that routine and, if so, how will you change it?

Do you belong to a gym or sports league, or participate in exercise classes and, if so, how frequently do you participate? If you do not participate in any of these activities, would you like to and, if so, what facilities would you like to join?

Do you enjoy exercising? If you need encouragement to exercise, would it be helpful for you to join a gym, find a workout buddy, or hire a personal trainer?

Do you like to play golf, tennis, or other sports? Do you have access to the necessary courses, clubs, or sport facilities? Do you know or have access to other players? If not, how could you find them?

The Health of Others

In addition to your own health, the health of your spouse, children, or other family members with whom you live or for whom you have responsibility will also affect your retirement choices.

Does your spouse/partner or other family member have any physical or emotional problems? If so, what impact will those problems have on your retirement options and plans?

Explore Your Feelings about Aging

Your attitudes and feelings about getting older can significantly affect your quality of life and your longevity. In one study, older people holding positive self-perceptions of aging lived on average 7.5 years longer than those with less positive views. A positive attitude reduces stress, including the mental stress associated with aging. Positive thinking about aging can also make you more resilient to illness and more proactive about your health.

How do you feel about getting older?

What will make you feel you are aging successfully?

How well are you coping with the aging process? For example, what do you worry about most or what frightens you about aging, and how do you deal with those feelings?

Have you discussed your feelings about aging with anyone? If not, would it be helpful for you to discuss these issues with a friend, family member, doctor, therapist, clergy member, or spiritual advisor? If you would like to speak to a professional about these issues but you don't know anyone, is there someone you can ask for a referral?

Who are the friends, relatives, neighbors, clergy members, and doctors you can turn to for emotional support?

Do you have emotional needs that are not being met now? If so, what are they and what will it take for you to address those needs in the future?

____

____

____

Do you feel angry or unhappy to the point it interferes with your ability to move forward toward a happy future? If so, what will need to happen for you to get beyond those negative feelings and move forward?

____

____

____

What kind of help can you seek to deal with any of these negative feelings? If you aren't sure, where could you find out? Whom might you ask?

____

____

____

Do you engage in yoga, meditation, mindfulness, or other practices to help you feel calm and manage stress and negative feelings? If not, would you like to learn more about these practices? What will you do to learn more?

____

____

____

Practice Gratitude

One way to counter negative feelings and promote wellness is to think about the things in life for which you are grateful. We often talk abstractly about "counting our blessings," but practicing gratitude means taking a deeper look at what those blessings are. Acknowledging and expressing gratitude for the many things you appreciate and are thankful for can lift your mood, inspire a sense of meaning and purpose, and increase your health, happiness, and overall well-being.

List at least ten things in your life for which you are grateful.

1. ______________________ 6. ______________________

2. ______________________ 7. ______________________

3. ______________________ 8. ______________________

4. ______________________ 9. ______________________

5. ______________________ 10. ______________________

Add to this list regularly.

Chapter Review

1. *This chapter explored various financial and health-related factors that may constrain the choices you make in your retirement planning. Describe the constraints you need to deal with.*

Financial constraints: ______________________

____

____

Your health constraints: ______________________

____

____

Health problems of others: ______________________

____

____

2. *Fill out the chart below.*

In the first column of the chart, list the constraints that might restrict your retirement options, such as positions you hold or family responsibilities. Think about what you will do to reduce, manage, or cope with those constraints. In the second column, describe the strategy you develop. You might want to enlist others to help you develop and/or execute your strategy. In the last column, list the kind of help you will need and where you might get it.

Constraint	Strategy	Sources of Help
Example: I want to take long trips but I'm responsible for my father's care.	• Persuade brother Ted to do it while I'm traveling • Use a home health provider • Get a college student to provide some care in exchange for free rent in Dad's house	• Brother Ted's wife • Look into home health services • Contact local colleges, look online, ask friends • Check if insurance or Medicare will cover any home health costs

3. *What have you learned about yourself in this chapter? List your five most important insights.*

1. ____________________

2. ____________________

3. ____________________

4. ____________________

5. ____________________

4. *What do your insights suggest about your choices for your future retirement?*

____

____

____

5. *List three to five decisions you have made or are considering about your retirement after completing this chapter.*

1. ____________________

2. ____________________

3. ____________________

4. ____________________

5. ____________________

Additional Notes and Action Items

Use this space to record additional notes or observations, as well any action items they inspire.

CHAPTER 8

GETTING YOUR LEGAL AND MEDICAL ARRANGEMENTS IN ORDER

> World Death Rate Holding Steady at 100 Percent.
>
> —HEADLINE IN *THE ONION*

Planning for retirement is a good time to get your legal and medical affairs in order. The retirement planning process focuses primarily on living a long, happy, and healthy life, but it is important to also consider what may happen to you as you age. At some point, someone may have to manage and distribute your estate, make decisions regarding your health care, and handle your affairs if you become incapacitated or die. For many people, talking *or even thinking* about these subjects is difficult, uncomfortable, or frightening. After all, acknowledging your mortality is not easy. Yet facing these subjects, and preparing yourself, family members, and agents or representatives in advance, can reduce the anxiety. It ensures that your wishes will be carried out regarding how you will be treated and how your estate will be handled. It also brings comfort and relief to know that the grief of your loved ones in the future will be eased by your thoughtfulness and organization now.

Many legal and medical documents require lawyers, but others do not. You can obtain some relevant information from various sources including AARP, bar associations, hospitals, agencies that deal with aging, and medical societies. However, because these documents have legal ramifications and the applicable laws are highly complex, it is wise to speak to a lawyer. Simple wills and some health care directives are available as online forms, many of them state-specific, but even those should not be filled out without an understanding of their legal implications. If you have a sizable estate, there may also be tax consequences to consider.

Some of the areas that have legal implications to think about during your retirement planning include: Social Security and Medicare, creating a will and/or estate plan, and preparing health care directives such as a living will. Below are some basic questions to help you start thinking about how to deal with them.

Key Ages to Consider in Retirement Planning

There are several key ages to keep in mind as you get closer to retirement, although your personal financial situation, the provisions of your retirement plans, and state and federal tax laws will determine your possible actions and ultimate decisions. Changes in the social security and tax laws may cause these ages to change, but as of 2019, these are the ages to consider:

- **Age 55:** You may withdraw some retirement plan savings without penalty if you are fired, laid off, quit, or retire from your job.
- **Age 59½:** You may withdraw money from qualified plans/IRAs without IRS penalty.
- **Age 62:** The earliest age when you may begin collecting Social Security.
- **Age 65:** You become entitled to Medicare coverage.
- **Ages 65–67:** You are entitled to full Social Security. (Depends on when you were born.)
- **Age 70:** Your Social Security benefits reach the maximum amount.
- **Age 70½ or 72:** You must start taking required minimum distributions (RMDs) from your retirement plans. (Depends on when you were born.)

SOCIAL SECURITY AND MEDICARE

Dealing with Social Security, Medicare, and other government benefit programs can be very complicated. There are many resources available to help you navigate those programs, including medicare.gov and ssa.gov.

 Apply for Social Security and Medicare

Do you understand when and how to apply for each of these benefits and, if not, what can you do to educate yourself? For example, will you attend a local seminar, talk to a friend or relative, or search for information online? Jot down your ideas below.

____

____

____

If you have not yet applied, do you understand the factors to consider in timing your decision, including income and tax implications, and have you decided when you will apply?

____

____

____

WILLS AND ESTATE PLANNING

To be sure that your estate will be distributed to the heirs you choose in the manner you want, you need to have a will. The larger your estate, the more important it is to have professional legal and financial assistance. Lawyers, financial planners, estate planners, insurance agents, and accountants are some of the professionals who can help you with issues related to will drafting, taxes, trusts, estate planning, government benefits, pension plans, and other financial affairs.

 Make a List of Your Professional Advisors

Use the table to list your advisors, their contact information (including address, phone number, and email address), and how they help you (e.g., estate planning, financial advice, tax preparation). Include any pertinent identifying information, such as documents prepared or policy numbers. Copy or transfer this information to a page you will make available to your spouse, family members, or representative.

Professional Advisor	Contact Information	Area of Assistance	Identifying Information

Do your spouse/partner and other family members know who your advisers are and how to reach them?

___

___

___

Do you have a will, codicils, a living trust, and/or an estate plan and, if so, have they been reviewed in the last five years?

___

___

___

What are the dates of your will and codicils, and where are the originals located?

1. Will/Codicil Date:________________ Location: ______________________________

Who has copies: ____

2. Will/Codicil Date:________________ Location: ______________________________

Who has copies: ____

3. Will/Codicil Date:________________ Location: ______________________________

Who has copies: ____

What are the dates of any trusts you have established, and where are the original trust documents located?

1. Date of Trust:________________ Location: ______________________________

Who has copies: ____

2. Date of Trust:________________ Location: ______________________________

Who has copies: ____

3. Date of Trust:________________ Location: ______________________________

Who has copies: ____

Do your spouse/partner and children have copies of your will, codicils, living trust, and/or estate plan or know where to find them?

____

____

____

If you have not yet created a will or estate plan, now is the time to do it. Begin by considering your legal heirs and any other people to whom you want to leave your estate. Who will have a right to inherit property in your estate (i.e., your legal heirs)?

____

____

____

Do you want any specific heirs to receive any particular assets? If so, list the assets you want to specify and who should receive each of those assets in the chart on page 162.

Are there other people or organizations to whom you want to leave bequests?

How recently have you updated the named beneficiaries in your insurance policies and retirement accounts?

Next, catalog everything you own, which will constitute your estate. Include the following assets if they apply to your situation:

- Homes and other real estate
- Personal property (e.g., cars, jewelry, art, collections, boats, computers, furniture)
- Financial assets (including savings and checking accounts, money markets, stocks and bonds, mutual funds, certificates of deposit)
- Retirement accounts (e.g., IRA, social security, pensions, 401(k))
- Insurance policies and annuities
- Intellectual property rights
- Military benefits
- Other

For every asset you own, list any pertinent information that will enable the asset to be found and accessed, such as the location of deeds and accounts, account numbers, issuers and policy numbers of insurance policies, brokers, lockbox keys, software programs (e.g., Quicken) and passwords for them. If you want to bequeath the asset to someone in particular, indicate the intended recipient in the fourth column.

Asset	Location	Identifying/Access Information	Intended Recipient(s)

Have you designated people who will act as the executor of your will and/or trustee of any trusts and discussed your wishes with them? If so, note who you selected below and, if not, note whom you will select and when you will discuss your wishes with them.

____

____

____

____

1. Name of executor: ______________________________

Date of will:______________ Location of document:______________________

Who has copies: ______________________________

2. Name of executor: ______________________________

Date of will: ______________ Location of Document: ______________________

Who Has Copies: ______________________________

3. Name of trustee:______________________________

Date of trust: ______________ Location of Document: ______________________

Who has copies: ______________________________

4. Name of trustee:______________________________

Date of trust: ______________ Location of Document: ______________________

Who has copies: ______________________________

If you have minor children, have you identified one or more people to act as guardians for them if necessary, and have you discussed your wishes with these potential guardians? Have they agreed? If you have not designated a guardian, indicate whom you will select and when you will discuss your wishes with them.

____

____

____

____

Are these guardians named in your will?

Date of will: ______________________________

If you have a pet, what arrangements will you make for its care? Where have you documented your wishes?

____

____

____

PERSONAL REPRESENTATIVES

Asking someone to be your personal representative for financial or medical affairs is a critical decision because that person will essentially speak and act for you when you are no longer able to do so for yourself. There are basic legal requirements for a personal representative. Some requirements vary by state, but in most jurisdictions they must be of the age of majority, of sound mind, and willing to act as your representative. In addition, while personal representatives for business or financial affairs need not be lawyers or finance professionals, it is helpful if they are knowledgeable about estate law, are comfortable with accounting, or have a financial background. Being detail-oriented, organized, responsible, and reliable is also helpful. And it is essential that they are comfortable in executing your wishes and managing on your behalf.

Your personal representative for medical decisions may face particularly delicate and emotional issues. Disagreements among family members and conflicts with medical personnel can exacerbate an already stressful situation. Most people name their spouse, partner, a relative, or a close friend as their health care agent. The most important factor in your choice is that the person knows you well and you trust him or her to carry out your wishes. This representative should also be assertive in dealing with medical personnel, able to handle stress and, if necessary, be able to manage difficult family dynamics and willing to make very hard decisions.

Select a Personal Representative for Financial Affairs

Have you designated a personal representative to execute your financial affairs (sometimes called an "attorney-in-fact") if you become unable to do so yourself? If so, note who you selected and if not, note when you will choose someone and execute the necessary power of attorney.

____

____

____

If you have selected a personal representative for financial affairs, have you discussed your wishes with that person, and have they agreed?

____

____

____

Have you executed a "financial power of attorney" naming that person as your personal representative? If so, state when was it executed and where that document is located. Does the designated representative have a copy?

____

____

____

1. Name: ____________________

Date of financial power of attorney: ____________ Location of document: ____________

Who has copies: ____________________

2. Name: ____________________

Date of financial power of attorney: ____________ Location of document: ____________

Who has copies: ____________________

MEDICAL DIRECTIVES

Certain legal documents state your health care preferences and provide directions about how you want to be cared for, treated, or managed in case of illness or incompetence.

A "Living Will" or "Advance Health Care Directive" (AHCD) is a document in which you designate your preferences for medical treatment. It outlines your wishes for what should happen when you are no longer able to choose or consent to certain treatments such as life-prolonging treatments, food and water, palliative care, and "do not resuscitate" (DNR) orders. You can put any wishes you have for medical care in your living will. You can instruct that certain types of care should be given or that certain types of care should be withheld. If your wishes in a certain situation are not known, your representative (named in your AHCD or a Durable Power of Attorney for Health Care) will make a decision based on what he or she believes you would want.

 Your Health Care Representatives

Have you designated someone to act as your health care representative or agent who will gather information, speak for you, and make decisions on your behalf if you become unable to do so? If so, note whom you selected below; if not, note when you will choose someone.

____

____

Have you discussed your wishes with that person? Have they agreed?

____

____

Note your medical directives, including the individual(s) you selected to be your representative for medical decisions, the date you executed each medical directive, location of the documents, and who has copies.

Durable Power of Attorney for Health Care

Representative: ____

Directive Date: ______________ Location of Document: ______________________

Who Has Copies: ____

Representative: ____

Directive Date: ______________ Location of Document: ______________________

Who Has Copies: ____

Living Will or Advance Health Care Directive

Representative: ____

Directive Date: ______________ Location of Document: ______________________

Who Has Copies: ____

Representative: ____

Directive Date: ______________ Location of Document: ______________________

Who Has Copies: ____

Have you discussed your wishes with your primary physicians and given them copies of the pertinent documents for your medical file?

Does your designated health care representative have copies of all pertinent documents?

Have you documented your preferences or wishes regarding your funeral (including financial arrangements for it) and disposition of your body? In which document is this information recorded?

If you have not yet created these medical directives, where can you obtain the information and/or assistance you need?

Chapter Review

1. *This chapter presented many legal and medical decisions to be made and documents to be prepared. The following checklist highlights some of them. Check off those you have completed; indicate the action you will take for those that remain to be done.*

❑ Write/review will and estate plan

❑ Execute financial power of attorney

❑ Execute medical directives

❑ Contact needed medical and legal professionals

❑ Find pertinent resources online

❑ Decide about/sign up for Social Security

❑ Decide about/sign up for Medicare

❑ Designate/talk with representatives

- ❑ Legal
- ❑ Financial
- ❑ Medical

❑ Designate/talk with Guardian for minor children

❑ Discuss all the above with spouse

❑ If unmarried, discuss with family or representative

❑ Others: ______________________________

2. *Do your spouse, partner, or representatives have sufficient information to manage your health care and financial affairs as you wish, should it become necessary for them to step in? Do they have what they will need in order to access your legal, medical, and financial documents and accounts if they have to (e.g., documentation, a key for items in a safe deposit box, passwords for online accounts)?*

____

____

____

3. *What have you learned about yourself in this chapter? List your five most important insights.*

1. ____
2. ____
3. ____
4. ____
5. ____

4. *What do these insights suggest about your choices for your future retirement?*

____

____

____

5. *List three to five decisions you have made or are considering pertaining to any legal or medical decisions that impact your retirement.*

1. ____
2. ____
3. ____
4. ____
5. ____

Additional Notes and Action Items

Use this space to record additional notes or observations, as well any action items they inspire.

CHAPTER 9

ENVISIONING YOUR FUTURE LIFE IN RETIREMENT

> Tell me, what is it you plan to do with your one wild and precious life?
>
> —MARY OLIVER

So far in this workbook, you have studied your present status, values, and history. You have also acknowledged the possible impacts and constraints related to retirement, and appreciated the steps to take to get your financial, legal, and medical affairs in order. Now, you can begin to envision and design the kind of retirement you hope to have. This chapter will help you imagine what that future might be. It examines your attitudes and desires about many common issues that come up when people think about retiring: the kinds of activities that will keep you busy; whether to continue working, either for pay or as a volunteer; where and how much you want to travel; and where you want to live. It then asks you to stretch your imagination about what your "ideal" future would actually look like.

CHOOSING WHAT TO DO WHEN YOU RETIRE

If you could do anything you wanted, what would you do? What would each day look like? Questions like these might have been theoretical once, but in retirement, you can shape your future to reflect your answers. You are free to decide and do what is most important to you. You may be faced with financial, health, family, or other constraints, of course. But without the stress of a job and the demands of bosses, patients, or clients, your desires are more likely to be realized than ever before.

The world is filled with fascinating and exciting things. Watching, inquiring, and being open to new ideas and unexpected opportunities will show you many possibilities that you may not have imagined before. And those possibilities are endless! They include hobbies, classes, travel, lessons, sports, art, music, dance, languages, caregiving, political activism, philanthropy, volunteering, technology—anything and everything that you might do, learn, or explore when you are able to choose how to spend your time.

The rest of this chapter will focus on five areas where retirement will present you with major choices:

- Will you continue to work for pay?
- What interests and activities will you pursue?
- Will you work as an unpaid volunteer?
- Will you travel?
- Where will you live?

The questions and exercises in this chapter will help you think through the issues and consider the possibilities before you make any decisions. If you have already decided, they might spark some new ideas to enhance your experience.

 Draw a Picture of Your Ideal Future

What would your ideal future life look like? What would make it interesting, enjoyable, and fulfilling? Start with the big picture—literally. On the facing page, draw it (or describe it) in as much detail as you can. As you create your image, consider various features:

- Where are you?
- Who is with you?
- What are you doing?
- What is going on around you?
- How do you feel?
- What are you wearing?
- What is the weather like? What's the temperature?
- What sounds do you hear?
- What can you smell?
- Do you feel any textures?
- Do you taste anything?

This is your chance to exercise your imagination. Don't hold back! Feel free to use words as well as drawings, sketches, photos, and pictures you cut from magazines. And if you want more space, use a large sheet of blank paper.

If you find it hard to start, don't worry about making it perfect. Take Picasso's advice: "To know what you're going to draw, you have to begin drawing." Plunge in; sometimes the very act of drawing will inspire the creation of a vision.

If you would like some verbal guidance to help you visualize your "ideal future," please visit the website for Retirement by Design, https://ulyssespress.com/rbd. You will be able to listen to directions and prompts while you close your eyes, relax, and envision your ideal future.

You may have many options and possible directions that generate different images, and as you move ahead, new ideas, opportunities, and choices will appear. It's fine for you to have more than one vision of your future life, and to revise your vision as circumstances change. Use additional pages for alternative visions.

THIS IS WHAT MY IDEAL FUTURE LOOKS LIKE:

WORKING FOR PAY IN RETIREMENT

Many people facing retirement have worked enough and are ready to stop. If that is your choice, there is plenty to keep you busy and engaged, including family, leisure, travel, and other non-work activities. Other people choose or need to stay in the workforce in some capacity. In fact, moving directly from full-time work to full-time retirement is becoming less common. Retired professionals in particular continue to do some sort of work in their field of expertise or another, for pay or as volunteers. Many of them start new "encore" careers and a large number of them are self-employed.

 Two-Week Work Log

If you are still working, keep a log in the section below of the best and worst parts of your job. For two weeks, write down the things you find most satisfying each day, as well as those you like the least. Use the pages below or a separate notebook or journal.

At the end of two weeks, review your notes. What did you learn about your current work that you want to keep in mind as you decide on any future activities?

WEEK 1: WHAT I LIKE / DISLIKE ABOUT WORK

Sunday	Monday	Tuesday	Wednesday	Thursday	Friday	Saturday
like:	like:	like:	like:	like:	like:	like:
dislike:	dislike:	dislike:	dislike:	dislike:	dislike:	dislike:

WEEK 2: WHAT I LIKE / DISLIKE ABOUT WORK

Sunday	Monday	Tuesday	Wednesday	Thursday	Friday	Saturday
like:	like:	like:	like:	like:	like:	like:
dislike:	dislike:	dislike:	dislike:	dislike:	dislike:	dislike:

Assess Your Current or Recent Work

What do you like the most about your current or most recent work?

____

____

____

What aspects of your work are okay, but not great?

____

____

____

What do you like least about your current or most recent work?

____

____

____

Side Hustles

Many people start a "side hustle," or work outside their regular job in order to make extra money or try out something that interests them before they retire. Have you considered a side hustle? If so:

- What kind of work would you like to try while you are still working at your day job?
- How much time will you spend on it? How will that impact your regular job?
- Will you need to make a financial investment? How much money will that require? How much can you afford?
- Is it something you could expand into a business when you retire?

What Kind of Future Work Do You Want?

If you want to continue working after you retire, what are the reasons you want to keep working?

____

____

____

Do you want to work full-time or part-time? How much time per week/month/year?

____

____

____

How much flexibility do you want in scheduling your work time? Rank your preferences on the list below.

____Set my own hours

____A set number of hours per week or month

____A set schedule each week or month

____Project-based work where I work steadily for a while, then take time off

____Consulting work, where I can control my commitments

____Other (describe)

Do you want to continue working in the same field or profession?

____

____

____

If it is an option, or if you could negotiate it, would you want to continue working in the same organization? If so, in what capacity would you like to work there? The same work and position you have now or something different? Part-time or full-time? Would you like a "phased retirement," gradually reducing your work commitment before you leave the job completely?

____

____

____

Do you want to continue in the same field or profession but in a different organization?

____

____

____

Would you like to work in the same field but doing something different from what you did before? For example, if you were in sales, would you prefer to be in product development?

____

____

____

Do you want to work in another field and if so, what field?

____

____

____

What is the basis of your interest in that field and what knowledge or experience do you have in that field?

____

____

____

Will you need to get additional education or training to do that work?

____

____

____

Do you know any people in that field who can give you information, contacts, or a job?

____

____

____

Would you prefer to work:

- ❑ On your own?
- ❑ With one or a few other people?
- ❑ For an organization?

What kind of organization would you like to work for (e.g., large company, nonprofit, small business, school, service organization)?

____

____

Would you prefer to work: ❑ At home?
❑ In an outside office?
❑ On the road?

Would you be willing to move to another location if necessary to pursue the work you desire?

❑ Yes ❑ No

Are there any job benefits or perks you want the job to provide (e.g., technology, paid vacation, sick leave, health insurance)?

____

____

How much responsibility do you want in your work?

❑ I want to be a leader (e.g., owner, chair, president, board member, team leader)

❑ I want to be a contributor with limited ongoing responsibility

❑ I want to be a worker bee, handling limited tasks

❑ I want to work on my own with responsibility only to clients

❑ I want to be a consultant

❑ Other: ____

If you want to be paid for your work, how much money do you want to earn?

____

How important is the amount of pay you receive?

❑ Very important; I want/need the income

❑ Moderately important; the extra income is desirable but not essential

❑ Not important; I want something for my effort, the amount doesn't matter

❑ Other: ____

How do you want to be paid (e.g. salary, commission, project basis)?

List all the means and sources you can think of to help you identify and apply for job opportunities. For example, will you reach out to recruiters? Contact companies directly? Use your network of contacts? Use school or firm alumni association resources? Search online job message boards? What else can you do?

Do you have an up-to-date résumé? If you need to write a new one, what will you emphasize that will make you an attractive candidate?

Freelancing in the Gig Economy

Many retirees who want to supplement their income work as freelancers or doing short-term work rather than taking permanent jobs. In most cases, the work is arranged through online platforms in what is sometimes referred to as the "gig" or "online platform" economy. Familiar gig jobs include driving for Uber or Lyft, doing jobs through Task Rabbit, renting out rooms and homes through Airbnb, and selling crafts through Etsy. Working "gigs" allows you to be your own boss and work only when and for as long as you want.

If this appeals to you, what kind of freelance or gig work would you like to do?

____

What kinds of skills, interests, or resources do you have that you could use in freelance work?

____

What will you do to learn about the opportunities that exist for you?

____

STARTING A NEW BUSINESS

Many people who retire start new businesses. People age 55 to 64 started a quarter of all the new businesses formed in recent years, and a US Census Bureau study showed that 60-year-olds are three times as likely to found a successful start-up than people half their age. Moreover, research finds that older business owners are more successful and that continuing to work helps their mental health.

People start businesses in retirement, or in preparation for it, for many reasons: to make money, stay active and busy, fulfill long-time interests, challenge themselves, utilize their expertise, leverage their skills, form new social networks, or seek renewed purpose in their lives. Many people continue the same work they were doing, but with greater autonomy or in a different way; they might offer freelance services, become consultants or start new firms.

The range of business ventures started by retirees covers every imaginable area of products and services. A few examples of successful businesses started by people in their 50s, 60s, and 70s include:

- Selling supplies for pottery making
- Producing software to help job seekers find jobs
- Designing clothing for people with limited mobility
- Opening a café and wine bar
- Starting a virtual law firm for retired lawyers
- Manufacturing keyboards and bar code scanners
- Producing and selling homemade jams and cookies
- Buying, renovating, and selling homes
- Managing and coordinating house moves
- Running a bed-and-breakfast
- Selling fine art online

- Buying and selling gold jewelry
- Security consultation advice and services
- Philanthropy for grandparents
- Writing and editing services
- Yoga instruction for older adults
- Being a theater critic for local newspapers
- Dog walking
- Personal shopping
- Tour guiding
- House sitting
- Landscaping
- Career coaching

Things to Consider When Starting a New Business in Retirement

If you would like to start your own business, what are your reasons for doing so?

____

____

____

What kind of business interests you?

____

____

____

Do you know this business or will you be learning something entirely new?

____

____

____

Have you ever started or owned your own business before?

What is your vision for the business?

Will you do it alone or with one or more partners?

How much time and money are you willing to invest and for how long?

Starting a Business

There are many questions to contemplate and many books and resources available to give you information and guidance about starting a new business, such as the US Small Business Administration (www.sba.gov). Some of the most important things to consider are noted below:

- Business planning
- Money for starting the business
- Financing for ongoing operations
- Staffing and personnel

- Marketing
- Production
- Legal requirements
- Technology
- Management
- Advisors
- How long it will take to be profitable
- The amount of time you will have to commit to building and running the business

How much risk can you tolerate?

___

___

___

What will be your role? Do you have the skills and knowledge you need to do the job?

___

___

___

Will you need any staff? What will they do? What skills and knowledge will they need? Where will you find them?

___

___

___

Where will the business be located?

What materials and resources will you need?

What do you know about potential competitors?

What market research will you do?

How will you market your products or services?

In addition to the US Small Business Administration, note below any other resources you can find to help you decide on and start your business.

In order to decide whether and how to start a business, list the following actions you will take:

Action you will take	Resources you will need	Target date

DESIRED ACTIVITIES, EXPERIENCES, AND PURSUITS

What kinds of activities, experiences, and pursuits would you like to engage in after you retire? The questions that follow will help you identify and clarify your choices by examining the things you love to do and the things you are doing now.

You might also review your answers from earlier chapters. Look for features of your life that you definitely want to continue or add in the future. Consider areas that remain unresolved or that you regret but can now deal with; areas that will help you achieve critical priorities, uphold important values, or fulfill your sense of purpose; areas that will establish your legacy or reflect the role you want to play in the world; and areas that will make life interesting and fun.

 What Do You Love to Do?

This is a good time to think about the things you love to do, that give you pleasure, or help you find meaning in your life. Consider the kinds of activities you enjoy or think you would enjoy if you had the time, energy, and resources to do them. Thinking about these things at this point in your life and from a retirement perspective can trigger new ideas and inspire you to move in new directions.

Use the table below to list what you love to do and things you would love to do, including past activities you would like to resume.

Things You Love to Do	Things You Would Love to Do

Things You Love to Do	Things You Would Love to Do

You likely engage in many personal activities, pursuits, and hobbies now. Note those activities below and consider which of them you want to continue when you retire and how much time you want to devote to them.

Activity:____

❏ Yes ❏ No *If yes, how much time?* ❏ Same amount ❏ Less time ❏ More time

Activity:____

❏ Yes ❏ No *If yes, how much time?* ❏ Same amount ❏ Less time ❏ More time

Activity:____

❏ Yes ❏ No *If yes, how much time?* ❏ Same amount ❏ Less time ❏ More time

Activity:____

❏ Yes ❏ No *If yes, how much time?* ❏ Same amount ❏ Less time ❏ More time

Activity:____

❏ Yes ❏ No *If yes, how much time?* ❏ Same amount ❏ Less time ❏ More time

Activity:____

❑ Yes ❑ No *If yes, how much time?* ❑ Same amount ❑ Less time ❑ More time

Activity:____

❑ Yes ❑ No *If yes, how much time?* ❑ Same amount ❑ Less time ❑ More time

Activity:____

❑ Yes ❑ No *If yes, how much time?* ❑ Same amount ❑ Less time ❑ More time

Activity:____

❑ Yes ❑ No *If yes, how much time?* ❑ Same amount ❑ Less time ❑ More time

LIFELONG LEARNING

One of the joys of retirement is being able to indulge a passion for learning. Whatever your interests are, there are countless opportunities to learn about them. Some colleges and universities allow retirees to audit regular undergraduate classes. Some host classroom-based "lifelong learning programs" designed specifically for older adults, with extensive curricula in a wide variety of subjects. These programs can be found through providers such as the worldwide Age-Friendly University network, or the Osher Lifelong Learning Institutes found on more than 120 college campuses across the country. Several universities offer semester or year-long residential programs where experienced individuals can study, reflect, and contemplate what they will do next. You can also study abroad or even at sea. The Semester at Sea Lifelong Learning Program provides adults age 30 and older the chance to study and travel with undergraduate students from around the world as part of an intergenerational "floating college campus."

Other sources of educational programming include professional associations, community centers, and public libraries. Educational courses of all sorts are available online as well. Learning online is convenient, but some online formats (e.g., viewing archived presentations) can be isolating.

 Continuing Your Education

Are you interested in continuing your education and, if so, what would you like to study?

____

____

____

Below are a number of different learning objectives. Elaborate on each objective that applies to you. For example, if you are intellectually curious, what would you like to learn about?

Intellectual curiosity ____

____

Intellectual stimulation ____

____

Complete studies you dropped earlier _________________________________

____

Explore new fields you might enter or pursue __________________________

____

Help you decide what to do next _____________________________________

____

Personal renewal and growth ____

____

Work toward a degree or certificate ___________________________________

____

Desire to study particular subjects ____________________________________

____

Pursue a passion ____________________

____

Update knowledge or skills ____________________

____

Develop new skills ____________________

____

Prepare for a new job/career ____________________

____

Other: ____________________

What kind of educational experience do you want? Use the space below each item to elaborate.

Occasional classes ____________________

____

Wide variety of classes ____________________

____

Classes following a set curriculum ____________________

____

Audit college classes ____________________

____

Take classes for credit ____________________

____

Degree program ____________________

____

Certificate program ____________________

____

Study abroad ___

___

Experiential learning (e.g., internship) ___

___

Adult education classes ___

___

Intergenerational classes ___

___

Online classes with live participation by video ___

___

Study groups ___

___

Private tutors ___

___

Work-study ___

___

Other ___

___

What educational providers and resources are available near you that offer the learning opportunities you desire?

___

___

If any learning opportunities that interest you would require you to move or travel, are you willing to do that?

____

____

Which online educational providers and resources provide the learning opportunities you desire?

____

____

Think about the types of classes and educational programs that interest you. For each, consider the following and note your thoughts:

Do you have the necessary qualifications? ______________________

What is the application process? ______________________

____

What is the cost to apply? ______________________

What is the cost to attend? ______________________

Is financial assistance available? ______________________

What is the time commitment? ______________________

What kind of technology will you need? ______________________

____

ACTIVISM AND VOLUNTEERING

Consider issues or things that you care about. Examples include children, sick or homebound individuals, animals, the environment, veterans, poverty, politics, diversity, education, immigration, or curing particular diseases. Given that you will have more free time when you retire, do you have certain skills or talents that you would like to apply to a nonprofit, social impact, or other organization where you might volunteer? Examples include caregiving, driving, tech support, accounting, mentoring, tutoring, leadership, fundraising, lobbying, filmmaking, translating, and writing.

 Getting Involved as a Volunteer

List below the organizations, clubs, associations, nonprofits, political movements, or other groups and causes that you are now involved in and whether or not you will continue your involvement when you retire. If you stay involved, note the future role(s) you see for yourself in the organization and if your involvement will increase, decrease, or stay the same.

Current Volunteer Activities

Organization/Cause ____________________

Continue? ❑ Yes ❑ No If yes, in what role? ____________________

____

How much time? ____________________

Organization/Cause ____________________

Continue? ❑ Yes ❑ No If yes, in what role? ____________________

____

How much time? ____________________

Organization/Cause ____________________

Continue? ❑ Yes ❑ No If yes, in what role? ____________________

____

How much time? ____________________

Organization/Cause ____________________

Continue? ❑ Yes ❑ No If yes, in what role? ____________________

____

How much time? ____________________

Organization/Cause ______________________________

Continue? ❑ Yes ❑ No If yes, in what role? ______________________________

____

How much time? ______________________________

If you want to stop or decrease your involvement, do you anticipate any resistance from the group?

❑ Yes ❑ No *If yes, how will you handle it?* ______________________________

____

Past Volunteer Activities

List below any organizations or causes you have been involved with in the past to which you would like to return in some way. State the role(s) you see for yourself, and indicate how you will contact the group to let them know of your interest.

Organization/Cause ______________________________

Return in what role? ______________________________

____

How/when to contact? ______________________________

Organization/Cause ______________________________

Return in what role? ______________________________

____

How/when to contact? ______________________________

Organization/Cause ______________________________

Return in what role? ______________________________

____

How/when to contact? ______________________________

Organization/Cause ______________________________

Return in what role? ______________________________

____

How/when to contact? ______________________________

New Volunteer Activities

If you would like to volunteer for something new, what causes or organizations interest you? List them below and indicate how you will learn more about the cause or organization. For example, will you look at their website, ask people who are involved with them, or visit and observe? Use the last line for notes about what you learn that will help you decide whether or not to get involved.

Organization/Cause ______________________________

Where/How to learn more: ______________________________

Notes: ______________________________

Organization/Cause ______________________________

Where/How to learn more: ______________________________

Notes: ______________________________

Organization/Cause ______________________________

Where/How to learn more: ______________________________

Notes: ______________________________

Organization/Cause ______________________________

Where/How to learn more: ______________________________

Notes: ______________________________

Organization/Cause ______________________________

Where/How to learn more: ______________________________

Notes: ______________________________

Organization/Cause ______________________________

Where/How to learn more: ______________________________

Notes: ______________________________

After considering the organizations and volunteer activities identified through the exercises above, list the possibilities that sound most appealing to you.

1. ______________________________
2. ______________________________
3. ______________________________
4. ______________________________
5. ______________________________
6. ______________________________
7. ______________________________
8. ______________________________
9. ______________________________
10. ______________________________

What kind of volunteer work do you want to do for these organizations or causes?

____

____

____

How much time do you want to devote to volunteer activities each week? Each month?

____

____

____

How will you apply for the volunteer work you want?

Do you have the necessary qualifications and if not, how will you acquire them?

Will you have to go through training? Do you know what it entails? Are you willing to do it?

Will you need an introduction to someone at the organization? Do you have a contact who can make one?

TRAVEL

Many people look forward to retirement as a time when they can finally take the trips they have deferred while they were busy with their careers and raising families. Even people who have done a good amount of travel may take advantage of more leisure time and fewer demands afforded by retirement to visit and revisit places in the world they want to see.

Planning to Travel

If you are looking forward to traveling, list the places you would like to go in order of priority and mark them on the map below.

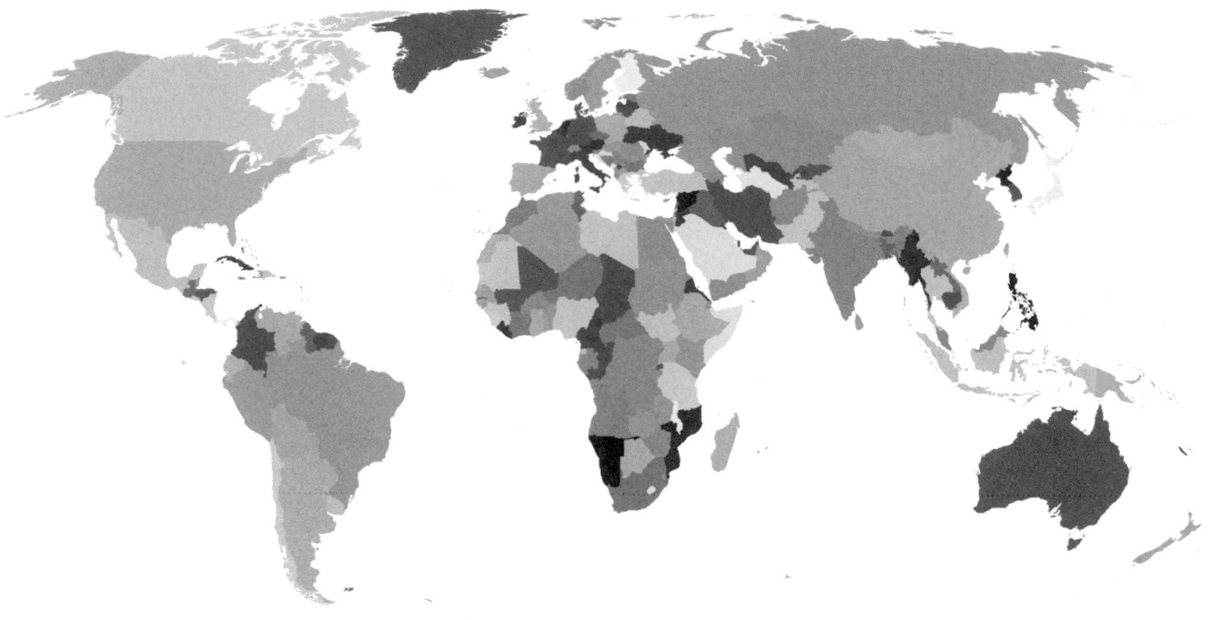

1. ______________________
2. ______________________
3. ______________________
4. ______________________
5. ______________________
6. ______________________
7. ______________________
8. ______________________
9. ______________________
10. ______________________
11. ______________________
12. ______________________

How experienced a traveler are you on a scale of 1 to 5, with 1 being "highly experienced" and 5 being "inexperienced?"

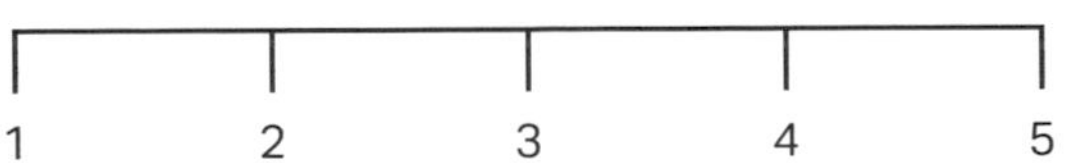

When, how often, and for how long will you travel each year?

Are there any factors or constraints that might prevent you from traveling?

Are there particular trips you might not be able to take because of health, political factors, responsibilities for other people, or other reasons?

What class of travel do you prefer (e.g., luxury, rustic)?

How will you travel (e.g., by air, cruise ship, bicycle, RV)?

Will you travel alone, with your spouse/partner, with friends, or with a tour group?

Would you like to live in another place for an extended period of time? If so, note some places that appeal to you and how long you would like to stay.

Would you like to do a home exchange and if so, what arrangements will you need to make for such a move?

Home Exchanges

Exchanging homes with other people can be a cost-effective way to travel. It allows you to visit and live in other places without the expense of house rentals or hotels. People swap homes not just for long holidays, but while visiting family or friends, or getting to know a place before moving or retiring there. If you are comfortable with having strangers live in your home while you live in theirs, this may be an option to consider. Several companies organize home swaps and some, like Home Exchange 50Plus and Seniors Home Exchange at International Vacation Home Exchange (IVHE), specialize in home exchanges for people over 50.

Would you like to study abroad and if so, what, where, and for how long would you like to study?

How will you find out what study opportunities exist there and what do you need to do to apply? What arrangements will you need to make in order to move abroad?

Would you like to do charitable volunteer work when you travel and, if so, what kind of work would you like to do and where would you like to go?

What will you need to do to find suitable opportunities? For example, do you know any organizations that sponsor volunteer work abroad and, if not, how will you find out what organizations there are?

If you plan to be away for extended periods, what arrangements will you need to make to care for your home and possessions while you are away?

WHERE WILL YOU LIVE WHEN YOU RETIRE?

Some retirees relocate in order to downsize for financial reasons, to be closer to family members (see sidebar page 118), or to live in more temperate climates. The next few questions are intended to help you determine whether you want to stay where you are when you retire or move somewhere else, and if you would like to move, to consider what the best move would be.

Things to Consider about Moving in Retirement

Do you plan to stay in the home where you live now? If so, will you do anything to make it more comfortable, accessible, or "livable" as you get older?

If your home is an apartment or is part of a homeowners' association, what permits or approvals will you need to make those alterations?

What factors would lead you to move to another home?

If you decide to move from your home, where would you move and would you build, buy, or rent?

Would you like to live part-time in more than one place and, if so, in which places?

What time of year and for how long would you live in each?

Have you factored the expense of multiple dwellings (including travel costs, rents or mortgages, taxes, utilities) into your retirement budget?

Intentional Communities

Intentional communities ("ICs") are designed to bring people together in living arrangements that foster both social connection and independence. Residents live separately but share resources and responsibilities. Many ICs are intergenerational, and some are built around particular shared values, such as environmental responsibility or economic equity. But many ICs are planned and designed as residential communities for older adults. In "Senior Co-Housing" or "Elder Intentional Communities," residents live independently and cooperatively. Neighbors look after each other as they age, sharing support and resources for caregiving, property and home maintenance, and transportation.

What type of housing would you prefer? Check the options that appeal to you.

- ❏ Single-family dwelling
- ❏ Townhouse
- ❏ Apartment building
- ❏ Condominium
- ❏ Intentional community
- ❏ Houseboat
- ❏ Ranch or farm
- ❏ Mobile home
- ❏ Assisted living facility
- ❏ Other ______________________
- ❏ Other ______________________
- ❏ Other ______________________

If you have not yet selected a location to live, list some places that sound appealing and what appeals to you about them. Include both domestic and international locations.

____

____

Have you spent any time as a resident or visitor in the places you have identified? If not, when do you plan to visit to see if you would like living there?

____

____

If You Live Abroad

If you decide to live outside the United States, will you move there permanently or just for a period of time?

____

What will it cost you to move abroad?

____

How will the cost of living abroad affect your retirement budget?

____

How often will you return to the United States?

What will you do with your current home and possessions if you move abroad?

What will you need to do to put your legal and financial affairs in order before you move abroad?

How will you receive your social security, pension, and any other retirement benefits while living abroad?

Will you have access to good and affordable health care? Which of your expenses will Medicare cover if you receive care abroad?

 Choosing the Best Place to Live

What will you do to investigate the desirability and feasibility of retiring to the places you are considering? The following exercise is a good way to start.

How important are the following factors in deciding about the community and location where you will live? For each factor, place a checkmark in the appropriate box.

Proximity to:

Children ❏ Important ❏ Neutral ❏ Unimportant

Grandchildren ❏ Important ❏ Neutral ❏ Unimportant

Parents ❏ Important ❏ Neutral ❏ Unimportant

Other family members ❏ Important ❏ Neutral ❏ Unimportant

Friends ❏ Important ❏ Neutral ❏ Unimportant

Other________________________ ❏ Important ❏ Neutral ❏ Unimportant

Location and Geography:

Climate and Weather ❏ Important ❏ Neutral ❏ Unimportant

Urban ❏ Important ❏ Neutral ❏ Unimportant

Suburban ❏ Important ❏ Neutral ❏ Unimportant

Rural ❏ Important ❏ Neutral ❏ Unimportant

Beach ❏ Important ❏ Neutral ❏ Unimportant

Mountains ❏ Important ❏ Neutral ❏ Unimportant

Desert ❏ Important ❏ Neutral ❏ Unimportant

Other________________________ ❏ Important ❏ Neutral ❏ Unimportant

Other factors:

Size of community ❏ Important ❏ Neutral ❏ Unimportant

Affordability ❏ Important ❏ Neutral ❏ Unimportant

Safety ❏ Important ❏ Neutral ❏ Unimportant

Easy to make new friends ❏ Important ❏ Neutral ❏ Unimportant

Senior or retirement community ❏ Important ❏ Neutral ❏ Unimportant

Intergenerational community ❏ Important ❏ Neutral ❏ Unimportant

Intentional community ❏ Important ❏ Neutral ❏ Unimportant

Arts and cultural activities ❏ Important ❏ Neutral ❏ Unimportant

Organized social activities ❏ Important ❏ Neutral ❏ Unimportant

Sports, outdoor recreation ❏ Important ❏ Neutral ❏ Unimportant

Golf courses ❏ Important ❏ Neutral ❏ Unimportant

Leisure activities ❏ Important ❏ Neutral ❏ Unimportant

Pace of living ❏ Important ❏ Neutral ❏ Unimportant

Restaurants ❏ Important ❏ Neutral ❏ Unimportant

Health care and hospitals ❏ Important ❏ Neutral ❏ Unimportant

College/university nearby ❏ Important ❏ Neutral ❏ Unimportant

Near an airport ❏ Important ❏ Neutral ❏ Unimportant

Ease of walking ❏ Important ❏ Neutral ❏ Unimportant

Public transportation ❏ Important ❏ Neutral ❏ Unimportant

Shops, dining, etc., in walking distance ❏ Important ❏ Neutral ❏ Unimportant

Ability to have pets ❏ Important ❏ Neutral ❏ Unimportant

Other________________________ ❏ Important ❏ Neutral ❏ Unimportant

If you want to retire abroad, there are numerous other factors to consider in addition to those that apply generally to your choice of where to live. How important are the factors listed below in your decision about where to live abroad?

Housing availability ❏ Important ❏ Neutral ❏ Unimportant

Ability to speak the local language ❏ Important ❏ Neutral ❏ Unimportant

Desire to learn another language	❑ Important	❑ Neutral	❑ Unimportant
English is widely spoken	❑ Important	❑ Neutral	❑ Unimportant
Cultural familiarity	❑ Important	❑ Neutral	❑ Unimportant
Cultural differences	❑ Important	❑ Neutral	❑ Unimportant
Cultural events, activities	❑ Important	❑ Neutral	❑ Unimportant
A community of expats	❑ Important	❑ Neutral	❑ Unimportant
Local cuisine	❑ Important	❑ Neutral	❑ Unimportant
Ease of travel to US	❑ Important	❑ Neutral	❑ Unimportant
Reliable wifi access, technology	❑ Important	❑ Neutral	❑ Unimportant
Driving requirements, restrictions	❑ Important	❑ Neutral	❑ Unimportant
Health care (availability, cost)	❑ Important	❑ Neutral	❑ Unimportant
Health insurance (availability, cost)	❑ Important	❑ Neutral	❑ Unimportant
Reliable banking system	❑ Important	❑ Neutral	❑ Unimportant
Justice system based on rule of law	❑ Important	❑ Neutral	❑ Unimportant
Political stability	❑ Important	❑ Neutral	❑ Unimportant
Visa and residency requirements, restrictions	❑ Important	❑ Neutral	❑ Unimportant
Income requirements	❑ Important	❑ Neutral	❑ Unimportant
Ability to find work	❑ Important	❑ Neutral	❑ Unimportant
Other______________________	❑ Important	❑ Neutral	❑ Unimportant

Circle and list separately, in order of importance, all of the factors you marked as "Important."

1. ______________________ 6. ______________________

2. ______________________ 7. ______________________

3. ______________________ 8. ______________________

4. ______________________ 9. ______________________

5. ______________________ 10. ______________________

11. ______________________

12. ______________________

13. ______________________

14. ______________________

15. ______________________

16. ______________________

17. ______________________

18. ______________________

19. ______________________

20. ______________________

Using that list, can you envision—or at least narrow down—any particular locations?

For your top two or three location choices, indicate what you know about them in each "Important" category. If you are missing information, write down what you will do to find out more. After you have collected enough information, write down the pros and cons of moving there.

Location 1: ______________________

Important factors known ______________________

Need to find out ______________________

Pros: ______________________

Cons: ______________________

Location 2: ______________________

Important factors known ______________________

Need to find out ______________________

Pros: ____

____

Cons: ____

____

Location 3: ____

Important factors known ____

Need to find out ____

Pros: ____

____

Cons: ____

____

Live There Before You Move There

If you have not lived in your top choices before, is it possible for you test your assumptions about them by living there for a month or longer? You can then decide more accurately whether it is a good idea to move there.

If you do live there for a while, try to live as you would if you were a resident, not a tourist. Instead of staying in a hotel, house-sit or rent an apartment or house similar to what you would like to live in if you move there. Spend your time doing what you imagine you would do there every day. Take your trip during the off-season to see how you would like living there year-round.

When your trial period is over, consider these questions:

What were your expectations about living in that locale?

____

____

____

In what way(s) did it meet your expectations?

What did you enjoy the most?

It what way(s) was it disappointing?

What were the biggest drawbacks?

After living there for a short period, do you still want to move there?

❑ Yes ❑ No

Chapter Review

1. What have you learned about yourself in each part of this chapter? List your most important insights about:

The things you want to do when you retire ______________________________

____

Your attitudes and desires about work ______________________________

____

Your attitudes and desires about volunteering ______________________________

____

Your attitudes and desires about travel ______________________________

____

Where you want to live ______________________________

____

2. What do your insights suggest about your choices for your future retirement?

____

____

____

3. List three decisions you have made or are considering about your retirement after completing this chapter.

1. ______________________________
2. ______________________________
3. ______________________________

Additional Notes and Action Items

Use this space to record additional notes or observations, as well any action items they inspire.

CHAPTER 10

ORGANIZING, PRIORITIZING, AND EXPLORING RETIREMENT POSSIBILITIES

> Invention...does not consist in creating out of void, but out of chaos.
>
> —MARY SHELLEY

Now that you have collected a lot of information and generated a host of ideas, what will you do with it all? To design a manageable retirement plan, it will be necessary to sort through that information and find the activities, experiences, and pursuits that are the most important and appealing to you. This will entail a process of organizing, narrowing down and prioritizing your ideas, exploring and testing them, and repeating those steps until you come up with the best design for your future.

What you have accomplished up to this point is the hardest part of the retirement design process, and you are about to enter the more fun, creative part. Chapter 1 explained that this workbook is based on principles of "design thinking" (see page 15). In design thinking terms, through the work you have done so far in this workbook, you have developed greater awareness of yourself, your spouse, and your family (*empathy);* envisioned possible retirement scenarios (*definition);* and generated lots of information and ideas for the elements of those scenarios (*ideation)*. In the steps to come, you will find or create ways to try out the most enticing elements (*prototyping)* and use that experience (*testing)* to decide which ones will become part of your life in retirement.

This chapter will help you look for patterns in the answers you have written throughout this workbook. It can reveal connections between and among your interests and activities that you may not be aware of and which can lead you to creative new possibilities. It then provides a framework using "Three Lists" for you to identify the things you definitely want to do, might want to do, and want to learn more about before you decide. And it suggests methods for investigating new opportunities that interest you and how to pursue them.

If you are clear about what you want to do, then the issue for you is setting priorities and organizing a schedule, as provided in Chapter 11. But if you are trying to figure out how to spend your time, this exploration can be an ongoing, meandering, and sometimes spiraling process, not a linear one. As you investigate, experiment, test options, and learn more about possibilities, you may discover and create new ideas, and your priorities and choices may change and change again. Don't let it frustrate you. Treat it as an adventure that allows you to learn more about yourself and the world.

LOOKING FOR PATTERNS AND CONNECTIONS

Review the notes, answers, drawings, and lists you have recorded throughout this workbook. Look for entries that are connected in some way to others or that reveal patterns, themes, commonalities, and overlaps. These patterns can help you "connect dots" and direct you to activities that will satisfy or expand your interests.

 Examine Your Notes

Here are some questions to consider as you review what you have recorded:

Do any of the interests or pursuits you have listed relate to each other? Have you spotted any patterns or connections? Note them below.

____

____

____

____

____

____

____

Is there a way you might combine interests? For example, if you want to travel and learn more about art, can you take an art class in Florence? If you love to knit and also want to do some community service work, can you organize a group of knitters to make scarves for the homeless? If you are an avid and knowledgeable sports fan, what about writing a sports column for a local paper or coaching a team at a local boys or girls club?

With whom have you discussed your ideas? Talking about these interests with one or more of your Personal Advisory Team members can help you find connections you might not otherwise see.

Your Three Lists

Continue the organization process by categorizing and creating three lists: Will-Do List, Possibility List, and Curiosity List. These lists will help you narrow your interests and rank them in order of priority. Refer back to your answers and notes in other chapters of this workbook to find possible entries. Consider items in every aspect of life and every area of interest.

Use the following pages to prepare your three lists. You can also use separate sheets of paper and Post-it notes, a whiteboard and markers, or lists created on your computer, which will allow you to move entries from one list to another more easily.

WILL-DO LIST: WHAT YOU WILL DO

Your Will-Do List should include the things you are sure you want to do, including both current and new activities. Limit this list to your definite, highest-priority items.

Activity/Experience	How Will You Make It Happen?	When Will You Start?

POSSIBILITY LIST: WHAT YOU MIGHT DO

Your Possibility List is for the things you have a strong interest in and think you would like to do but aren't sure about and need to give more thought. Include things you have always wanted to do but didn't have time for, that you used to do but had to stop, or that once seemed exciting but you were afraid to do or were prevented from doing. Keep these entries on the Possibility List while you investigate, consider, and decide whether to act on them. If you do decide to go forward with something on this list, move it to your Will-Do List.

Activity/Experience	Why It Interests You	What You Need to Know Before Deciding

CURIOSITY LIST: WHAT YOU MIGHT EXPLORE

Your Curiosity List can include anything that sounds interesting or intriguing. Include as many things as you want on this list and add to it whenever you hear about something that sparks your curiosity. Don't worry about being practical or realistic; let your imagination run wild! Do you want to learn to sail, become a flamenco dancer, open a winery, get an advanced degree? With little at risk, this is the time to be bold, stretch, and experiment. You can explore the items on this list whenever you are looking for new ideas or inspiration, and as your interest in any of the items grows stronger, you can move them to the Possibility or even the Will-Do list.

Item to Explore	Why It Interests You	What You Want to Learn About It

GOING DEEPER: EXPLORING NEW POSSIBILITIES

Many of the items on your Three Lists are well known to you, but others will require some research. You will undoubtedly have too many items on these lists to explore them all at once, so you will have to narrow them down. For this portion of your investigation, focus on items on your Possibility and Curiosity lists.

Begin by selecting three to five of the most promising activities and experiences from your Possibility List and one or two items from your Curiosity List. For each of these items, think of how you can "test" the idea to determine whether you want to pursue it. The main question is what specifically do you want to learn about it? What information will help you decide whether this is something you want to do?

To gather information about topics, activities, jobs, organizations, opportunities, and anything else you want to learn about, make use of the many resources that are available to you. What can you find online? Where can you visit? What books can you read? Who can you call? This last question is especially important, as your network of contacts can be your best source of answers. Consider all the potential sources of information and conduct your research as you would on any other subject. If possible, see if you can attend a meeting or class, observe someone engaged in the activity, or try something out on a trial basis.

 Items to Investigate

Below, list the items you have selected from your Possibility and Curiosity lists, and for each, the key questions you want to have answered. Then try to ascertain and list as many possible sources of information as you can.

Item	Questions You Want Answered	Possible Sources
1.		
2.		
3.		

Item	Questions You Want Answered	Possible Sources
4.		
5.		
6.		
7.		

USING YOUR NETWORK TO INVESTIGATE NEW POSSIBILITIES

Sometimes the best source of information is people who do or know about what you are interested in. In trying to learn about or experience possible jobs, activities, programs, opportunities, or anything else, think about the people you know personally, professionally, or socially who might be able to help you. And don't stop there! Even if they are not knowledgeable or involved, they may have friends or relatives who are. If you know that they have useful connections, ask for an introduction.

Networking Is About Relationships

Networking is about building relationships that are honest, sincere, and of value to both parties. You might think of networking as a "career-boosting" practice, but it is important in retirement, too. By nurturing and expanding your network of friends, acquaintances, and contacts, you improve the chances of remaining active, engaged, and connected—and reduce the chance of becoming bored or isolated. Moreover, when looking for guidance about what to do in retirement, your network can be an excellent source of information, introductions, and support. Reaching out to your contacts for assistance offers many benefits:

- Your conversations will teach you new things, expand your thinking, and spark new ideas.
- You will gain credibility and build self-confidence by preparing well and communicating clearly.
- You will acquire leads and suggestions that may bring you closer to your goal or take you in exciting new directions.
- You will stay in touch with active connections and refresh relationships that may have languished.
- You may find unexpected opportunities as you discuss your interests and objectives.

Keep in mind that networking is mutual. When you seek help from your contacts, look for ways you can benefit them as well. At the very least, you might introduce them to people in your network who share their interests or meet their needs.

 Use Networks to Learn about Your Interests

For subjects and areas that you want to learn about, identify possible contacts and connections. In the table below, note the subject area, people you know who are knowledgeable about the subject or who might know someone else who is knowledgeable about it, and how and when you plan to reach these people.

Before you reach out to anyone, decide in advance what you want to learn from them and write that in the chart as well. For example, what does the activity involve? Can you shadow them to see what they do firsthand? Do they know of a volunteer opportunity for you for a week, month, or longer?

Subject	Your Contact	How/When to Reach Out	What to Learn

Keep Track of Your Efforts

As you explore, keep track of what you do to investigate, the people you speak with, what you learn and conclude, any follow-up actions you plan to take, and the outcome of your efforts.

Subject Investigated: ______________________________

Source/Person ____________________ Date of Information____________________

Next Steps: ____

____

Outcome/Decision ____

Subject Investigated: ____

Source/Person ____________________ Date of Information ____________________

Next Steps: ____

____

Outcome/Decision ____

Subject Investigated: ____

Source/Person ____________________ Date of Information ____________________

Next Steps: ____

____

Outcome/Decision ____

Subject Investigated: ____

Source/Person ____________________ Date of Information ____________________

Next Steps: ____

____

Subject Investigated: ____

Source/Person ____________________ Date of Information ____________________

Next Steps: ____

____

Outcome/Decision ____

Subject Investigated: ____________________

Source/Person ____________________ Date of Information____________________

Next Steps: ____________________

____

Outcome/Decision____________________

Subject Investigated: ____________________

Source/Person ____________________ Date of Information____________________

Next Steps: ____________________

____

Outcome/Decision____________________

THE BEST WAY TO LEARN: DIRECT EXPERIENCE

The best way to make good decisions about activities to pursue is through direct experience. Doing something is far better than reading, talking, or thinking about it. It allows you to learn firsthand what the activity is like and to test your hopes and expectations against reality. In addition to your mental processes, your physical, sensory, and intuitive impressions will tell you whether it's a good choice for you. It's like learning to ride a bicycle. You can study the instructions all day long, but to know if you'll be able to stay on and make it go, you need to get on the bike and give it a try.

Here are three examples of how to get personal experience in areas you want to learn about:

- Do you wonder if you'll like working in a nonprofit? If so, volunteer for a short-term project in a nonprofit organization you care about.
- Are you thinking about teaching a community college class? If so, ask if you can shadow one of their faculty members for a day or two.
- Would you like to become a political activist? If so, call the headquarters of an official you support and ask for a role in their political action committee or re-election campaign.

 Firsthand Experiences

List three to five possibilities you would like to experience first-hand. For each, describe what you will do to obtain that experience.

Possibility 1:____

Experience you want:____________________________________

How you'll get it: ______________________________________

Possibility 2:____

Experience you want:____________________________________

How you'll get it: ______________________________________

Possibility 3:____

Experience you want:____________________________________

How you'll get it: ______________________________________

Possibility 4:____

Experience you want:____________________________________

How you'll get it: ______________________________________

Possibility 5:____

Experience you want:____________________________________

How you'll get it: ______________________________________

After you try out an experience, assess the reality against your expectations. Here are some questions to ask yourself for each possibility noted above:

What did you expect from this possibility?: __________________________

____

Was the experience about what you expected? ❑ Yes ❑ No ❑ Better ❑ Worse ❑ Undecided

What are the reasons for your answer? ______________________________

____

Will you include this activity in your retirement plans? ❑ Yes ❑ No ❑ Undecided

What did you learn or discover during this experience? ______________________________

____

____

____

Chapter Review

1. *What have you learned about yourself in this chapter? List your five most important insights.*

1. ______________________________
2. ______________________________
3. ______________________________
4. ______________________________
5. ______________________________

2. *What do your insights suggest about your choices for your future retirement?*

____

____

____

____

____

3. *List three to five decisions you have made or are considering about your retirement after completing this chapter.*

1. ______________________________

2. ______________________________

3. ______________________________

4. ______________________________

5. ______________________________

Additional Notes and Action Items

Use this space to record additional notes or observations, as well any action items they inspire.

CHAPTER 11

PUTTING TOGETHER THE PIECES: DESIGNING YOUR RETIREMENT PLAN

How we spend our days is, of course, how we spend our lives.

—ANNIE DILLARD

At last you're ready to create a plan for what your days and weeks will look like. What will you choose to do? It is easy to become overwhelmed if you pick too many activities or if you pick activities that put excessive demands on you. But making good, thoughtful choices will help you lead a meaningful, balanced, and diversified life in retirement.

As you choose from among the many possibilities you have identified, remember that you can commit to something now; do some research and decide later; or try things out before making any decisions. And you can change your mind. If you don't enjoy what you're doing or are disappointed by a choice you made, you can switch to something else instead.

This chapter will ask you to rank in order of preference your desired activities and pursuits. Further narrowing those areas to a few things you would like to do daily, and others you want to do occasionally, will help you design a schedule of activities that will produce the greatest meaning and enjoyment for you.

Although you may work on this chapter alone, it is very important to bring a spouse or life partner into the process at this point if you have not done so before. Your long-term plans and daily schedule will affect both of you directly. New plans and schedules may create tensions that did not exist before. It is essential to have open and honest conversations about your mutual dreams and plans so that if they diverge, you will be able to work out your differences before anything becomes set.

Set Priorities for Action

As you rank your choices, consider some fundamental big-picture questions. Of the many possible activities and experiences you are considering...

...which would be most meaningful?

...which support the values most important to you?

...which would be the most fun for you?

...which arouse your passions?

...which will help fulfill your purpose in life?

...which would let you use your talents and strengths?

...which would engage you the most?

What will be a comfortable pace for you? Will your desired activities keep you busy enough? Too busy? Not busy enough?

If you take on work and/or volunteer responsibilities, how committed do you want to be? How much flexibility do you want? How much freedom do you want?

How much structure do you want in your schedule? Will your desired activities provide enough structure? Too much? Too little?

Will you have enough energy and stamina to carry out all of your desired activities? If you can't do them all, which are the most important to you?

When do you want to start? Do you want to first take six months to just relax and do some "creative loafing"? Do you want to jump right in and remain as busy as you are now? Do you want to ease into retirement, testing a few activities and building your plan slowly without any timetable?

INCLUDING VITAL ACTIVITIES IN YOUR PLAN

The categories of activity listed below are vital to your ongoing satisfaction and well-being in retirement. Be sure to include activities that will provide all these features in your retirement plan.

- Intellectual stimulation
- Social engagement
- Exercise and play
- Creativity
- Sense of purpose/Feeling useful

Some activities fall into more than one category, which is a nice bonus. Joining a hiking group is exercise and social; taking a writing class is intellectual and creative; planning a fundraiser for a cause that is dear to you can be purposeful, social, and creative.

CREATING YOUR RETIREMENT PLAN

Below are some exercises and templates to help you create your retirement plan. Keep in mind that a retirement plan does not necessarily look like a traditional project plan, with specific goals and timetables. You certainly can create a plan structured like that, either for your overall retirement or for specific projects within your overall plan. And if a goal-focused planning format is what you prefer, the simple template provided below will help you. You can also find more structured planning forms online and in project management books.

But a plan for retirement needs to be fluid and adaptable because retirement can last a long time, there are numerous variables, both known and unpredictable, and the older we get the more we can expect the latter. So this workbook suggests using a "scheduling" approach to design your retirement. Instead of a linear plan toward a specific goal, it encourages you to design an ideal but flexible schedule of activities and events that will help you enjoy life in retirement that is as busy, diversified, fulfilling, and enjoyable as you desire.

USING A TRADITIONAL GOAL-FOCUSED APPROACH

If you prefer a more structured plan for specific retirement goals, or for specific projects during retirement, you can use the following template. For each goal, describe your general strategy, or how you expect to achieve the goal. Indicate the action steps that will move you toward your goal; the resources (including people) you will need to achieve the goal; possible obstacles and how to overcome them; and a projected timetable.

Be as specific as possible. This will allow you to take more deliberate and focused action steps. As an example, let's say you are hoping to find a job. Can you define the kind of job you are looking for? If you state your goal as "getting a job as a human resources technology consultant," it will be easier to identify and narrow the steps you will need to take to find it.

Make sure your goals are also realistic and achievable, and give yourself a specific timetable for achieving them. Setting a goal that is a stretch for you is fine. In fact, it's a good idea. You may be 70 but you can still learn to tap dance or become an expert on Italian wines. Yet you also need to be realistic. If you are tone deaf, it is unlikely you will become a concert violinist—at any age. Moreover, having a timetable is important even if there is no urgency about when you reach the goal. It will keep you moving forward toward completion, even if the deadline keeps shifting.

Because retirement is not time-limited, you will likely have many new goals and undertake new projects as time goes on. You may have several plans in action at the same time and at various stages of completion. Whenever you have a new objective, you can use the template below to map it out by detailing the action steps and strategies you will follow to achieve it.

Goal-Focused Planning Template

Include the following information for each goal you set. Make copies of the templates if you need more.

Retirement/Project Goal: ______________________________

Overview of strategy for achieving the goal:

____

____

Deadline or timeframe for achieving the goal: ______________________________

Milestones or action steps along the way, including deadline or timeframe for each:

1. ______________________________
2. ______________________________
3. ______________________________
4. ______________________________

Resources you will need and how you will find them:

______________________________ ______________________________

______________________________ ______________________________

______________________________ ______________________________

______________________________ ______________________________

People who can help you:

Possible obstacles and how you will overcome them:

USING A SCHEDULING APPROACH: DESIGNING WITH A CALENDAR

Instead of moving step by step toward a particular goal, a schedule-based approach looks at the bigger picture and treats the goal—your ideal days, weeks, and years—as a flexible target. Think of it like a kaleidoscope. There are many moving parts and you can rearrange them to form different patterns until you find the one you like best. That will be the pattern of activities and events that constitute the best schedule for you.

The following exercises use a calendar-based planning approach. You will need a large blank calendar or other surface to work on, such as a whiteboard or butcher paper, along with Post-it notes that you can reposition and experiment with in various combinations. You can also use scheduling apps such as calendar programs or other software that afford both structure and flexibility. These apps may also send you reminders and notifications about your activities. But for many people, doing these exercises by physically moving pieces around, at least when you start, amplifies the sensation and enjoyment of creating and designing a plan.

Software Applications

Many people find it helpful to use software applications to facilitate scheduling, organizing, and managing tasks and projects. These apps fall into many categories, such as scheduling apps, productivity tools, digital to-do lists, and task management systems, and many are free, at least for basic versions. While they each have different advantages and utilities, some common features include the ability to schedule tasks and activities; map out projects and goals; capture and organize ideas, thoughts, and images; highlight priorities; set target dates; schedule appointments; make and attach notes; generate automatic reminders; monitor progress; and review completed tasks. Some popular software choices in this area include Evernote, Trello, Todoist, OneNote, and MyLifeOrganized.

As you fill in your calendars, leave some time for spontaneity. Things will come up unexpectedly, new opportunities will appear, and new interests will grab your attention. Consider your retirement plan a framework, not a straitjacket. Build in flexibility so that you can make adjustments when needed.

Over time, as your choices and priorities change, repeat this selection process with new activities.

From the various activities and interests you hope to pursue, create lists of those you will do on an ongoing or occasional basis. Ongoing activities may be daily (e.g., exercise every day) or weekly (e.g., volunteer as a mentor twice a week). Occasional pursuits include things like travel or attending concerts that you will do from time to time.

Top 10 Ongoing List

List up to 10 items to include in your regular daily or weekly activities. List them in order of preference, with #1 ranking the highest.

1. ______________________
2. ______________________
3. ______________________
4. ______________________
5. ______________________
6. ______________________
7. ______________________
8. ______________________
9. ______________________
10. ______________________

Top 20 Occasional List

Choose up to 20 items that you would like to do from time to time. List them in order of preference, with #1 ranking the highest.

1. ______________________
2. ______________________
3. ______________________
4. ______________________
5. ______________________
6. ______________________
7. ______________________
8. ______________________
9. ______________________
10. ______________________
11. ______________________
12. ______________________
13. ______________________
14. ______________________
15. ______________________
16. ______________________
17. ______________________
18. ______________________
19. ______________________
20. ______________________

Visualize, Try, Reflect

Visualize an ideal day for yourself in retirement. What would you do?

____

____

____

____

Take a day off from work (not a weekend day) and try it out. Afterward, reflect on your day. What did it feel like? Did it live up to your expectations?

CALENDAR-BASED PLANNING

The following exercises will ask you to create your retirement schedule directly on a calendar. Working with Post-it notes on a large, blank calendar will give you plenty of space and the ability to move entries around easily. The first exercise focuses just on the major activities that will fill up your days. The second exercise has you provide more details and helps you see a more complete picture of what your days and weeks might look like.

Start by planning your days for one week, then continue the exercises for a second week or a full month. Expanding the exercises to a longer time period will allow you to fit more of your Top 20 Occasional List items into your plans. It will also provide a better overview of all your activities and help you see where you might want to make adjustments.

Which Activities Will Fill Your Days?

Referring to the entries on your Top 10 Ongoing List and Top 20 Occasional List, fill in each day on your calendar for one week with your desired activities for that day

When you have done that, step back and see how this plan looks and feels to you. Examine each day individually as well as the week as a whole. Is this schedule too crowded? Not busy enough? Weighted too heavily in some areas and too lightly in others? Missing activities in an important aspect of life? Make any necessary deletions, additions, or adjustments to reach the degree of diversification and balance you want.

You won't really know if these are "ideal" days until you try them out. When you do, you may decide to make changes. As you move ahead, continue to make periodic adjustments so that you maintain a comfortable level of activity.

Design Your Schedule in Greater Detail

The previous exercise for designing your week-long daily calendar focused on your major activities. You might also want to fill in the calendar with more details of daily life. Here is a method that will help you see a more complete picture of what your days might look like. Using a large blank calendar and Post-its, follow the steps noted below.

1. Write each item from your Top 10 Ongoing and Top 20 Occasional lists on a separate Post-it note.
2. On additional Post-it notes, write in any chores and routine activities that will take up some of your time (e.g., morning coffee and newspaper, grocery shopping, laundry).
3. In the upper-right corner of each Post-it, mark the amount of time you expect that activity to take.
4. For any activities that will recur during the week, make the needed number of duplicate Post-its.
5. Organize your Post-its according to the time the activities will take. Put all the 30-minute activities together, one-hour activities together, and so on.
6. On a large, blank calendar, arrange the Post-its to fill in your daily activities for a week. This process will produce a more granular look at your schedule because it includes both mundane and major activities. Study this proposed schedule to determine whether it is comfortably balanced. Is it too busy or hectic in some areas or on some days? Are some important areas given too little time? Move around the Post-its to try out several variations until you come up with a daily and weekly schedule that looks good to you. Try it out for a while, see how it works, and revise as you go along, until you achieve a schedule you are happy with.

Assess Your Activities

After you try out a new weekly schedule, assess its reality against your expectations. Ask yourself the following questions about each major activity you have undertaken.

What did you expect by putting this activity into your schedule?

How did the reality compare to your expectations in terms of:

The nature of the activity	❑ What I expected	❑ Better	❑ Worse
The time it required	❑ What I expected	❑ Better	❑ Worse
The energy it took	❑ What I expected	❑ Better	❑ Worse
The intellectual stimulation it provided	❑ What I expected	❑ Better	❑ Worse
What you learned	❑ What I expected	❑ Better	❑ Worse
The engagement you felt	❑ What I expected	❑ Better	❑ Worse
The sense of satisfaction you hoped for	❑ What I expected	❑ Better	❑ Worse
The fun you had	❑ What I expected	❑ Better	❑ Worse

Is this an activity you want to repeat? ❑ Yes ❑ No

Will you keep this activity in your retirement plan? ❑ Yes ❑ No

Will you modify this activity in some way? ❑ Yes ❑ No

What will you change?

___

___

___

What did you learn or discover from doing this activity?

___

___

___

YEAR-LONG PLANNING

An annual calendar can help you plan for activities that will take more time to plan or will not fit into a daily or weekly routine. For example, if you are thinking of moving, taking a vacation, or looking for a new job, you might want to plot those things out on a year-long calendar. When you enter them on the calendar, it will be easier to see how much time you will need to allot for them, how some plans will interfere with others, and how some priorities will need to shift to accommodate them.

The Month in Review

1. After you have put your plan into effect for about a month, assess what is working well, what is not, and new areas to be considered. Look back on the last week and answer the following questions:

What went well? ______________________________

____

What was the high point of your week? ______________________________

____

What did you like most? ______________________________

____

What was the most meaningful thing you did? ______________________________

____

Were there any pleasant surprises? ______________________________

____

Were there any disappointments? ______________________________

____

Were there any problems? Do you think the problems can be fixed or will resolve over time?

____

____

Were you comfortable with the pace and energy demands of your schedule?

Do you see opportunities for growth in what you are doing?

What are you looking forward to doing next week?

Is there something you want to do more of?

Is there something you want to stop doing?

Is there something else you want to do instead?

Do you see any new and promising opportunities?

Do you want to be busier? Do you want to do less?

YOU'RE READY TO GO

Congratulations! Through your hard work and creativity, you have designed a plan to guide you into retirement. Your plan will help you shape your future and adapt to changes that occur in your life. Be sure to revisit it at least annually to assess how it is working, and more frequently as adjustments are needed.

As you move through this new stage of life, write down your experiences, observations, feelings, and reflections about retirement in this workbook or a separate journal. That way you can record and process what you go through as you actually make the transition into retirement. Noting your thoughts may also help you realize you need to make changes. Later, your notes can be a reference point to revisit any lingering challenges, develop new coping strategies, review what you have accomplished, and celebrate the progress you have made.

You can keep daily, weekly, or occasional notes. Some points you might want to write about are:

- What you accomplished
- What you decided
- What you are excited about
- What you are grateful for
- People you met/spoke with
- What you learned
- How you are feeling
- Concerns you have
- What you need to finish
- What you are looking forward to
- What you are planning next

Throughout your journey, be sure to stay in touch with members of your Personal Advisory Team. Many of them will continue to be helpful to you in the long term, not just while you are planning or transitioning into retirement. Plus, when you complete your transition, your experience will enable you to advise and support them—and others—when they want to design their own retirement!

Additional Notes about Your Retirement Plan

Use the space below to record additional notes or observations about your retirement, as well any action items they inspire.

RESOURCES

AGING/AGEISM

Books

Ashton Applewhite, *This Chair Rocks: A Manifesto Against Ageism* (Celadon Books, 2019)

Louise Aronson, *Elderhood: Redefining Aging, Transforming Medicine, Reimagining Life* (Bloomsbury Publishing, 2019)

Alan Castel, *Better with Age: The Psychology of Successful Aging* (Oxford University Press, 2018)

Atul Gawande MD, *Being Mortal: Medicine and What Matters in the End* (Metropolitan Books, 2014)

Lynda Gratton and Andrew Scott, *The 100-Year Life* (Bloomsbury, 2016)

Mary Pipher, *Women Rowing North: Navigating Life's Currents and Flourishing as We Age* (Bloomsbury Publishing, 2019)

Susan Avery Stewart, Ph.D., *Winter's Graces: The Surprising Gifts of Later Life* (She Writes Press, 2018)

Websites

Aging for Life

www.agingforlife.org

Aging for Life's mission is to help make Americans more informed, engaged, and conscious about aging.

National Institute on Aging

www.nia.nih.gov

NIA, which is part of the National Institutes of Health, leads a broad scientific effort to understand the nature of aging and to extend the healthy, active years of life. Provides information on an extensive array of topics including exercise, nutrition, dementia, and end of life issues.

Pass It On Network

www.passitonnetwork.org

This global network promotes positive aging.

Senior Planet

seniorplanet.org

You'll find information and resources that support "aging with attitude," with articles about news, health, sex and dating, technology, art and design, style, travel, and entertainment

Stanford Center on Longevity

http://longevity.stanford.edu

Accelerates and implements scientific discoveries, technological advances, behavioral practices, and social norms so that longer lives are healthy and rewarding

DESIGN THINKING

Bill Burnett and Dave Evans, *Designing Your Life: How to Build a Well-Lived, Joyful Life* (Knopf, 2016)

EDUCATION AND LEARNING

Lifelong Learning Programs

Age Friendly Universities

https://www.geron.org/programs-services/education-center/age-friendly-university-afu-global-network

This is a network of universities throughout the world that commit to ten principles, which include widening access to higher education and enhancing the lives of older members of their community through innovative educational programs, research, curriculum development, online education, health and wellness activities, arts and culture programs, and civic engagement opportunities

Fromm Institute

fromminstitute.org

Lifelong learning classes are held at the University of San Francisco (USF) in San Francisco.

Harvard Institute for Learning in Retirement

hilr.harvard.edu

Boston area learners can take classes through HILR.

Institute for Retired Professionals, The New School

www.newschool.edu/institute-for-retired-professionals

Continuing education classes are held at The New School in Manhattan.

Oasis Lifelong Learning

www.oasisnet.org/home

Offers programming that promotes lifelong learning, active lifestyles, and volunteer engagement in more than 250 communities around the US.

Osher Lifelong Learning Institutes

www.osherfoundation.org

On campuses of 123 colleges and universities around the US.

"Next Career" University Programs

Year-long residential educational programs that provide space and time for study and personal exploration, renewal, and growth.

Advanced Careers Initiative, University of Minnesota

umac.umn.edu

Advanced Leadership Initiative, Harvard

advancedleadership.harvard.edu

Distinguished Careers Institute, Stanford

dci.stanford.edu

Inspired Leadership Initiative, Note Dame University

https://ili.nd.edu

TOWER Fellows Program, University of Texas, Austin

https://towerfellows.utexas.edu

Online Classes

Coursera

www.coursera.org

EdX

www.edx.org

Masterclass

www.masterclass.com

The Open University on iTunes U

www.open.edu/itunes

Udacity

www.udacity.com

FINANCES

Budgeting and Tracking

AARP Retirement Home Budget Analysis

www.aarp.org/money/budgeting-saving/home_budget_calculator.html

Excel

templates.office.com/en-us/retirement-financial-planner-tm04022385

Intuit Mint

www.mint.com

Quicken Plan for Retirement

www.quicken.com/personal-finance/retirement

TIAA

www.tiaa.org/public/offer/insights/tools-calculators

Financial Planning

Emily Guy Birken, *The Five Years Before You Retire* (Adams Media, 2014)

Chris Farrell, *Purpose and a Paycheck* (AMACOM, 2019)

Jane Bryant Quinn, *How to Make Your Money Last: The Indispensable Retirement Guide* (Simon & Schuster, 2017)

Larry E. Swedroe and Kevin Grogan, *Your Complete Guide to a Successful & Secure Retirement* (Harriman House, 2019)

Managing Retirement Decisions, Society of Actuaries

www.soa.org/resources/research-reports/2012/research-managing-retirement-decisions

This series of briefs addresses a variety of retirement decisions with practical considerations and advice.

New Retirement

www.newretirement.com

Extensive financial information, calculators, and tools for retirement planning.

US Department of Labor

www.dol.gov/sites/default/files/ebsa/about-ebsa/our-activities/resource-center/publications/taking-the-mystery-out-of-retirement-planning.pdf

The Department of Labor publishes *Taking the Mystery Out of Retirement Planning*, a free 63-page booklet to help people 10 years away from retirement do financial planning. It contains many helpful worksheets.

The Money Alert

www.themoneyalert.com

Financial information and advice on many aspects of financial issues and retirement planning.

HEALTH AND FITNESS

Health in Aging

www.healthinaging.org

The American Geriatrics Society operates this website that provides health information for older adults and caregivers.

Medline Plus

medlineplus.gov/olderadulthealth.html

News and information on adult health topics in a site maintained by the US National Library of Medicine. Includes interactive Health Check Tools to help you check your health.

Senior Living Options

www.seniorliving.org/health

This website provides information and reviews resources related to health care issues and needs of older adults.

INDEPENDENT LIVING

AARP Livable Communities

www.aarp.org/livable-communities/about

Supports the efforts of neighborhoods, towns, cities, and rural areas to be great places for people of all ages to live in.

Aging in Place

www.aginginplace.org

Helps seniors, their family members, and their caregivers prepare their homes and their lives for successful aging in place.

Senior Living Options

www.seniorliving.org/housing

Website provides information and reviews resources related to housing issues and needs of older adults. Also addresses assisted living and long-term care facilities.

The Village Movement

www.helpfulvillage.com/the_village_movement

Local "villages" formed by and for older adults who want to remain at home, stay active and independent, and stay engaged in their own neighborhoods.

Village to Village Network

www.vtvnetwork.org

Provides support and resources that enable community members to build and sustain thriving Villages.

INTERGENERATIONAL FOCUS

Marc Freedman, How to Live Forever: *The Enduring Power of Connecting the Generations* (PublicAffairs, 2018)

The Age of No Retirement

www.ageofnoretirement.org

This network is working to build an age-neutral, intergenerational, and united society.

The Eisner Foundation

eisnerfoundation.org

Awards, funds, and advocates for innovative programs that unite multiple generations for the enrichment of communities.

Gen2Gen

generationtogeneration.org

A campaign mobilizing adults 50+ to stand up for and with young people.

Generations United

www.gu.org

The goal of this organization is to improve the lives of children, youth, and older people through intergenerational collaboration, public policies, and programs. The 2018 research-based report called "All in Together: Creating Places Where Young and Old Thrive," describes several intergenerational "shared site" programs.

Sages and Seekers

www.sagesandseekers.org

Bringing together seniors and young adults to build communities through conversation.

Semester at Sea

www.semesteratsea.org/lifelong-learner

Study as part of an intergenerational "floating college campus."

INTERNATIONAL FOCUS

Government Information about Living Abroad

Social Security Administration

"Your Payments While You Are Outside the United States," www.ssa.gov/pubs/EN-05-10137.pdf

US State Department on Retiring Abroad

travel.state.gov/content/travel/en/international-travel/while-abroad/retirement-abroad.html

Information and planning steps to take before retiring abroad.

Opportunities for Volunteer Work and Study

Abroad Reviews

abroadreviews.com

Forum for public reviews of international study and volunteer and intern programs.

Cross Cultural Solutions

www.crossculturalsolutions.org

Arranges international volunteering opportunities.

Fly for Good

www.flyforgood.com

Discounted fares for travelers who work or volunteer in international humanitarian work.

Global Volunteers

globalvolunteers.org

One, two, and three-week international service and learning programs.

GoOverSeas.com

www.gooverseas.com

Information about culturally immersive programs, trips, and jobs of all kinds around the world.

Peace Corps

www.peacecorps.gov

Peace Corps doesn't have an age limit—they're looking for people who are 50+.

Points of Light

www.pointsoflight.org

International program connecting volunteers with the causes they care about to inspire and lead change in communities around the world.

LEGAL INFORMATION AND FORMS

These websites have information and forms for wills, trusts, and estate planning.

FindLaw

estate.findlaw.com

LegalZoom

www.legalzoom.com/articles/estate-planning

Nolo

www.nolo.com/legal-encyclopedia/wills-trusts-estates

Rocket Lawyer

www.rocketlawyer.com/article/estate-planning.rl

MEDICAL INFORMATION AND FORMS

Health Care Directives and Living Wills

AARP

Advance Care Directive forms by State, www.aarp.org/caregiving/financial-legal/free-printable-advance-directives

FindLaw

estate.findlaw.com/living-will.html

Mayo Clinic

www.mayoclinic.org/healthy-lifestyle/consumer-health/in-depth/living-wills/art-20046303

Living wills and advance directives for medical decisions. Discussion of purposes and considerations of different directives.

Nolo

www.nolo.com/legal-encyclopedia/living-will-power-attorney-advance-directive-30023.html

Rocket Lawyer

www.rocketlawyer.com/article/living-wills,-health-care-power-of-attorney,-and-advance-directive.rl

MEDICARE

Medicare

www.medicare.gov

AARP

AARP offers Medicare Made Easy, a guide to choosing health care coverage at www.aarp.org/health/medicare-insurance/info-2018/medicare-made-easy.html.

Books

Philip Moeller, *Get What's Yours: Maximize Your Coverage, Minimize Your Costs* (Simon & Schuster, Inc., 2016)

MID-LIFE

Books

Angeles Arrien, *The Second Half of Life: Opening the Eight Gates of Wisdom* (Sounds True, 2007)

William Bridges, *Managing Transitions, 25th Anniversary Edition: Making the Most of Change* (Da Capo Lifelong Books, 2017)

Chip Conley, *Wisdom at Work: The Making of a Modern Elder* (Currency, 2018)

Marc Freedman, *The Big Shift: Navigating the New Stage Beyond Midlife* (PublicAffairs, 2012)

Jonathan Rauch, *The Happiness Curve* (Thomas Dunne Books, 2018)

Newsletters

Ageist

www.weareageist.com

Ageist is building a global movement of people over 50 who plan to live longer and better lives than ever before.

Next Avenue

www.nextavenue.org

This newsletter contains news and information for people over 50.

Next for Me

nextforme.com

News, resources, and events for people over 50.

Sixty and Me

sixtyandme.com

Newsletters, articles, and miscellaneous resources for women over 60.

NONPROFIT BOARD POSITIONS

BoardnetUSA

www.boardnetusa.org

Matches people seeking board positions with nonprofit boards looking for members.

PLANNING SOFTWARE

Evernote

evernote.com

MyLifeOrganized

www.mylifeorganized.net

OneNote

If you have Microsoft Office 365 you can use OneNote at products.office.com/en-us/onenote/digital-note-taking-app?rtc=1

Todoist

todoist.com

Trello
trello.com/en-US

RETIREMENT (GENERAL)

Books

Mitch Anthony, *The New Retirementality*, Fourth Edition (Wiley, 2014)

Mark Evan Chimsky, *65 Things to Do When You Retire* (Sellers Publishing Inc., 2012)

Jeri Sedlar and Rick Miners, *Don't Retire, Rewire! Third Edition* (Alpha, 2018)

Steve Vernon, *Retirement Game-Changers* (Rest-of-Life Communications, 2018)

Websites

AARP
www.aarp.org

"Disrupt Aging" is their motto. The website contains a vast array of resources that reflect the breadth of their work, which covers almost everything related to life after 50, including retirement.

Respectful Exits
www.respectfulexits.org

Modernizing retirement and making it more flexible.

Retirement Revised
retirementrevised.com

Edited and published by journalist and author Mark Miller, this website contains articles and resources on many different aspects of retirement, including career planning, investing, health care, and housing.

Newsletters

AgeBuzz
www.agebuzz.com

News, information, and opinion on retirement and all aspects of aging.

Lustre
www.lustre.net

Variety of short articles for women about modern retirement.

RETIREMENT PLANNING FOR COUPLES

Roberta Taylor and Dorian Mintzer, *The Couple's Retirement Puzzle: 10 Must-Have Conversations for Creating an Amazing New Life Together* (Sourcebooks, 2014)

Maryanne Vandervelde, *Retirement for Two* (Bantam, 2005)

SOCIAL CONNECTIONS

Meetup

www.meetup.com

Sets up meetings in many communities throughout the US based on shared interests. Individuals can join a local group to meet people, try something new, or do more of what they love.

ROMEO: Retired Old Men Eating Out

www.romeoclub.com

Social club for men, with chapters in many cities.

Senior Forums

www.seniorforums.com

Online community for meeting seniors around topics of shared interest.

Senior Living Options

www.seniorliving.org/online-dating

Discussion of online dating sites for older adults

Stitch

www.stitch.net

A member-driven worldwide community that helps people over 50 find companionship through local activities and events, online discussions, and travel.

The Transition Network

www.thetransitionnetwork.org

A community of professional women, 50+, whose changing life situations lead them to seek new connections, resources, and opportunities.

SOCIAL SECURITY

Social Security Administration

www.ssa.gov

Includes numerous publications, calculators, planners, and other helpful resources including:

- an estimator to determine your retirement benefits (www.ssa.gov/benefits/retirement/estimator.html)
- My Social Security, a way to open and manage your personal account online (www.ssa.gov/myaccount)

AARP

www.aarp.org/retirement/social-security

AARP Social Security Resource Center covers numerous aspects of Social Security.

Laurence J. Kotlikoff and Philip Moeller, *Get What's Yours: The Secrets to Maxing Out Your Social Security* (Simon & Schuster, Inc., 2016)

VOLUNTEERING/PUBLIC SERVICE/SOCIAL IMPACT

AmeriCorps Seniors Corps

www.nationalservice.gov/programs/senior-corps

A federally sponsored organization that offers volunteers the opportunity to do everything, from foster grandparenting to renovating homes.

CatchaFire

www.catchafire.org

Matches skilled professional volunteers with nonprofits to help them increase their capacity and achieve their missions.

Create the Good

createthegood.aarp.org

An AARP site that connects you with volunteer opportunities to share your life experiences, skills, and passions in your community.

Elders Action Network

www.eldersaction.org

Movement of "vital elders" working intergenerationally for social and economic justice, environmental stewardship, and sound governance.

Experience Corps

www.aarp.org/experience-corps

Fights poverty by tutoring elementary students to improve their reading (sponsored by AARP).

Idealist

www.idealist.org/en

Connects idealists—people who want to do good—with opportunities worldwide for action and collaboration.

SCORE

www.score.org/about-score

Sponsored by the US Small Business Administration, volunteers mentor small business owners in skills like finance, technology, and accounting.

Volunteer Match

www.volunteermatch.org/volunteers

Matches volunteers with more than 90,000 nonprofit organizations around the world.

Weave: The Social Fabric Project

www.aspeninstitute.org/programs/weave-the-social-fabric-initiative

Sponsored by The Aspen Institute, this is a project, or movement in the making, to replace loneliness, division, and distrust with relationship, community, and purpose.

WORK

Encore Careers

Marci Alboher, *Encore Career Handbook* (Workman Publishing Company, 2012)

Nancy Collamer, *Second-Act Careers: 50+ Ways to Profit from Your Passions During Semi-Retirement* (Ten Speed Press, 2013)

Encore

encore.org

Second acts for the greater good. People 50+ helping solve some of our biggest social problems.

Retirepreneur

retirepreneur.com

Encore careers for executives over 50.

Entrepreneurship

Dorie Clark, *Entrepreneurial You: Monetize Your Expertise, Create Multiple Income Streams, and Thrive* (Harvard Business Review Press, 2017)

Kerry Hannon, *Never Too Old to Get Rich: The Entrepreneur's Guide to Starting a Business Mid-Life* (Wiley 2019)

US Small Business Administration

www.sba.gov

Work for Yourself at 50+

https://workforyourself.aarpfoundation.org

AARP Foundation program, including workshops and resources, for older adults with limited income to explore options for self-employment and increase their financial stability.

Freelancing

Diane Mulcahy, *The Gig Economy* (AMACOM, 2016)

These websites post jobs for freelancers:

Fiverr

www.fiverr.com

Guru

www.guru.com

UpWork

www.upwork.com

Jobs After 50

Kerry E. Hannon, *Great Jobs for Everyone 50+* (Wiley, 2012)

AARP Learn@50

https://learn.aarp.org

Free educational programming on many subjects, including job search skills, résumé building, and interviewing.

ReServe, Inc.

www.reserveinc.org

Matching talented people 50+ with government and social services agencies for part-time work at a modest hourly stipend.

Retirementjobs

retirementjobs.com

Job search site for people over 50.

Virtual Career Network

www.vcn.org/index.php

For people aged 50+, provides information about careers and helps them find training and jobs.

Workforce50

www.workforce50.com

Has job listings and information to help navigate a job search or a search for a new direction.

Side Hustles

Side Hustle Nation

www.sidehustlenation.com

Information for an online community of people who want to grow a side hustle into a business.

SideHusl

sidehusl.com

Researches, reviews, and rates online platforms, and helps older workers ("vintage experts") find jobs and make money in the gig economy.

ACKNOWLEDGMENTS

The seeds for this book were planted five or six years ago during conversations about career paths with clients and colleagues who started to wonder when and if they would retire. I invited several of these people to lunch simply to discuss ideas about their "next act." Their ages ranged from the early 50s to the late 60s and they did not know each other, but it soon became clear that they shared many questions and concerns, even though their specific situations varied widely. A few of the people at that lunch decided to continue meeting, and since I agreed to facilitate the sessions, I began to research retirement-related subjects so that I could offer the group helpful resources and more intelligent guidance. That research, those discussions, and the materials I drafted for the group, became the foundation for this workbook and grew into a new area of my practice. My sincere thanks to the members of that group for their inspiration.

I'am deeply grateful to the dozens of clients, colleagues and friends who have shared their retirement stories, struggles, joys and insights with me. In particular, a big thank-you to Rob Riesenfeld, my good friend, former physician, and tap-dance partner, and his wife Rosemary, for setting such a good example of how a well-thought-out plan can lead to a happy and fulfilling retirement.

There are several people whose help led to the publication of Retirement by Design, especially Sandra and Richard Gilbert, who hosted the dinner that set the networking process in motion; Keith Riegert and his team at Ulysses Press, who made the book a reality; and professional colleagues who offered advice, encouragement, expertise, and a willingness to answer questions or offer platforms for trying out ideas, including Nora Riva Bergman, Susan Saltonstall Duncan, Joan and Mark Feldman, Ari Kaplan, Aileen Leventon, Linda Marks, Sonia Menon, Bill Migneron, Barbara Riess, Ann Jenrette Thomas, Tim Smallsreed, Marilyn Tucker, and Rachel Zoffness.

My husband, Myles Abbott, deserves much of the credit for this book. His wisdom, patience, and superb editing skills helped me craft it, and his love, as always, carried me through.

ABOUT THE AUTHOR

Ida Abbott is a leader in the field of talent management and an internationally recognized expert in the areas of mentoring, sponsorship and the advancement of women into leadership. Over more than four decades as a lawyer and consultant, her practice has focused on the power of mentoring relationships to guide, support, and transform professional careers from the beginning of practice through retirement. Today she applies her talents to help firms improve retirement processes and to serve senior professionals as a retirement mentor and coach.

Ida co-Founded the Professional Development Consortium and the Hastings Leadership Academy for Women, and has held leadership positions in numerous professional organizations in the United States and globally. In recognition of her lifetime contributions to the legal profession, she was elected a fellow of both the American Bar Foundation and the College of Law Practice Management. Ida is a popular speaker and the author of several seminal books and publications, including *The Lawyer's Guide to Mentoring*, Second Edition, and *Sponsoring Women: What Men Need to Know*. She and her husband live in Oakland, California. Learn more at www.IdaAbbott.com.